From Zero to Hero in Your Finances

Dr. Richard Knapp

Uncle Richard

II Cor 9: 8

First published by Dog Ear Publishing
4010 W. 86th Street, Ste H
Indianapolis, IN 46268
www.dogearpublishing.net

dog ear
PUBLISHING

ISBN: 978-1-4575-1044-1

This book is printed on acid-free paper.

Printed in the United States of America

Illustrations by David M. Knapp, davidmknapp@gmail.com, © 2012 David M. Knapp

pressing into God. You contributed greatly to this book project with editing and with lots of creative input including the idea for the "heroes'" testimonies. You always believed in me even when I didn't. We are most blessed that the Lord chose to use *you* in our lives!

Thank you, Marsha Reed, for your generous application of loving and creative advice and ideas. We appreciate all the hours you put into this book!

David, our precious son, we are so thrilled that you were willing to illustrate this book. You did a great job, and we are so pleased and proud!

Finally, thanks to all the "heroes" who took the time to write down the wonderful stories of the miraculous provision of God in your lives. Your testimonies make this book come alive—*"the testimony of Jesus is the spirit of prophesy."* Rev. 19:10[2].

Richard Knapp, M.D.
November, 2012

ACKNOWLEDGEMENTS

In giving honor to whom honor is due, first of all I want to bless our wonderful Lord, who called forth this book and has enabled us all along the way. Father, you have always been faithful and have blessed us beyond what we could think or imagine.

I want to thank my parents, Doug and Evelyn Knapp, who laid their lives down unreservedly on the mission field for 28 years in Tanzania and provided an incredible example of love, dedication and faith. I am so grateful for the tremendous legacy I have received from you. I am sure, Dad, that it was your generous provision for me as I grew up that has enabled me to learn to trust my Heavenly Father for the same. Also, thank you, Daddy, for being the first editor of the very rough initial manuscript of this book and for your valuable insights and suggestions. I suspect Mother is sipping tea as she reads it in her new mansion!

Martha, my beloved wife, you have stood by my side for nearly thirty years, through thick and thin, and without you this book certainly would not have happened! You have gone with me to the office or to wherever we could get away, for countless hours, helping me with the book and encouraging me. Your editing skills have been invaluable. Thanks for always believing in me, being a sounding board and for being a team with me.

We are most grateful to our pastor, Dr. H. Mack Ballard. You have been a tremendous encourager and a wonderful example of generosity, integrity, passion, accountability and faithfulness. You continually spur us on in our own spiritual growth by your lifestyle of

Dr. Richard Knapp has been a friend of mine for twenty years and we have come to know each other like two soldiers who have been together fighting a war. I have been his Pastor now since 1992 and have watched him mature in every area of his life, but nowhere has he advanced more than in the area of giving and stewardship.

This book will take new Christians into the realm of stewardship in a fresh, non-threatening way. Also, more mature believers will identify some areas of stewardship where they may make improvements. There is one thing for sure, anyone who reads this book WILL see refreshing information and experience enlightening challenges to their psyche about finances and provision.

Dr. H. Mack Ballard
Senior Pastor
Ft. Revival Community Church
Ft. Mitchell, Alabama

TABLE OF CONTENTS

Well digging

1.

DIGGING WELLS

The hospital administrator came into my office and took the seat by my large mahogany desk. Almost immediately, he handed me an envelope addressed simply: "Dr. Richard Knapp, Director, Department of Pathology." My mind began to reel as I read: "I'm sorry to inform you that according to our Contract dated . . . we are activating the ninety-day termination clause effective today." My mind immediately flashed over to my wife and four young children, and the rising quagmire of hospital politics. Then I heard the administrator speaking and forced myself to listen. "Of course we may have trouble replacing you, so we would like you to continue to work for thirty days at a time after the ninety days if you haven't found another job." I nodded numbly, knowing that the job market for pathologists was at an all-time low.

When he left, I cried out to the Lord. "What's going on, Lord? Surely this isn't from You?" but got no answer. I remembered that the Lord had clearly spoken seven years before that He was sending me to this town (not to the job). I knew I wouldn't be able to leave until He released me, and that there were no other pathology jobs locally.

We fought to keep the job, but lost. I tried to get other jobs within commuting distance, but none were available. I went ahead and searched over the whole southeast U.S. for a job, but reached a dead end. Our savings were used up first, and then we began to live on the small amount of retirement money we had painfully put aside, paying the ten percent early withdrawal penalty. We actually started a small pathology lab, which helped pay for my malpractice insurance, but produced no real income. Months turned into years and my faith that God would take care of us was at an all-time low. Bankruptcy seemed a not too distant reality.

One day during my (now longer) devotions, the Holy Spirit brought to my mind a message we had heard years before entitled "Don't Let the Devil Throw Dirt in Your Wells". Wells symbolize God's provision and blessing. Abraham dug many wells, which were later filled with dirt by the Philistines, a type of the enemy. Isaac, Abraham's son, had to dig the dirt out of the wells despite opposition from the Philistines.

> *Genesis 26:18-19,22:* *[18]Then Isaac dug again the wells of water which had been dug in the days of his father Abraham, for the Philistines had stopped them up after the death of Abraham; and he gave them the same names which his father had given them. [19]But when Isaac's servants dug in the valley and found there a well of flowing water, [20]the herdsmen of Gerar quarreled . . . . [22]He moved away from there and dug another well, and they did not quarrel over it; so he named it Rehoboth, for he said, "At last the LORD has made room for us, and we will be fruitful in the land."* [3]

> *Isaiah 12:2-3:* *²Behold, God is my salvation; I will trust, and not be afraid: for the LORD JEHOVAH is my strength and my song; he also is become my salvation. ³Therefore with joy shall ye draw water out of the **wells of salvation.***[4]

The Hebrew word used here for salvation is *yeshuah* (Strong's 3444) and is one of the words for Jesus. It means essentially the same as the Greek word for salvation, *soteria*. Both words not only mean to be saved spiritually (from sin and from hell), but also to be rescued from danger and fear, to safety and security; from moral corruption to personal holiness; from sickness to health; and from poverty to prosperity. In each area of salvation it is our responsibility to dig the well. When a well has been properly dug, the water flows freely into it. The water from a functional well will always be available, not only to us, but to others around us. The devil, however, will constantly try to throw unbelief into our wells to dry up our faith in that area.

When I had heard the message, the Lord had spoken to me about my well of healing, and I knew I needed to dig in that area. My wife and I had thought that we had the well of provision reasonably well dug. Now I realized that my well of salvation, in the way of faith for God's financial provision, had failed. It had simply dried up. I asked the Lord about it, and He revealed to me that there are shallow wells and deep wells. I had possessed a shallow well that would work when the water table was high, but would fail in a time of drought. He wanted me to develop a deep well extending down into the rock, a well that would never fail. I felt impressed to develop a collection of scriptures relating to God's promises of provision. These were to help dig my well of salvation for supernatural provision. The Lord also seemed to indicate that this tool would not just be for our own lives, but would help other believers as they faced financial crises in their lives.

In preparing this collection, we have used multiple resources, some of which were exhaustive in the area of God's principles of finance. We discovered that there are a huge number of scriptures relating to finances, with many different and diverse pertinent subtopics. This book, however, is designed to provide a compact reading program specifically to build faith in the area of belief for God's provision.

As we studied the scriptures, we began to feel the return of our faith in God's care for us, like water to a wilted plant. We found multiple warnings in scripture about weaknesses and sins in our lives that affect God's provision for us. We feel it necessary to include several of these topics, because overcoming certain weaknesses was vital to us in receiving God's blessing on our finances. Part of digging the well of God's provision involved embedding scriptural principles into our hearts. These truths were then available so that the Holy Spirit could use them to warn and convict us. We are slowly changing to be more like Him. We will relay some of the stories of how He convicted us, changed us, and provided for us throughout this book. We will also intersperse others' stories of God's provision to encourage you.

God wants us to be whole persons. He also knows what motivates us, and for me at least, finances provide a significant motivation. For instance, I learned that the Lord will treat me in the financial realm the way I treat my wife in the same area (Rev. 19:7, Rev. 21:9, Gal. 3:7). As a result, I became much more generous with her. I didn't want to have God always putting me on an extremely tight budget because of my stinginess with my wife! I also learned that financing believers who are living in serious unrepentant moral compromise is a sure way to see my own finances dry up (II John 1:7-11, Eph. 5:5-7)!

Digging the well for God's provision must impact our *motives*. We have therefore provided a brief instruction at the beginning of each topic. The introductions include real-life examples and explanations about pitfalls of attitude that may keep one from experiencing the full blessing of God. Most sections also conclude with a prayer of confession. Prayer brings us into the presence of the living God where the Spirit purifies our hearts and motives.

It is important to know that our definition of prosperity does not fit the secular meaning. We believe true prosperity begins with an ability to pay our obligations (by paycheck, savings or grace). Some may argue that it also presumes that we have followed the Lord's leading in making those purchases and commitments. Prosperity further implies an *ability and willingness* to *give* at every opportunity and to every cause *for which the Holy Spirit prompts us*. I have learned that God does not muzzle the ox, or in this case, the giver (I Timothy 5:18). When He is providing for me to finance the kingdom of God, there will also be enough left over to meet my own needs and often, many of my (sanctified) wants.

God loves to bless His children in practical ways, but He cares much more about our character and our relationship with Him. We must learn to trust His goodness and His desire to bless us. At the same time we must learn not to let finances control us or make us feel overly important in our own eyes.

Digging a well is an active spiritual process, not a passive mental one. Of course, your use of this guide will be tailored to your personal needs and time constraints, but we thought it wise to let you know how its use was originally envisioned. As you have read, its purpose is to work into your soul and spirit the faith to believe God for finances, and the character and lifestyle that will allow Him to bless you. The character aspect involves bringing your motives and actions into line with God's laws, so that you're always working with and not against the Lord.

For most people, the book will best fulfill its purpose if read regularly, perhaps daily, in short segments. It is divided into 25 individual devotions to allow it to be read in a month. There are interspersed testimonies of Heroes of the Faith whose stories of trials, victories and most of all, the faithfulness of God will encourage you. God *is* faithful in real-life circumstances, and He is *good*! You may well wish to reread this volume over several months, perhaps as many as six times. As you ponder these scriptures, the Holy Spirit will quicken different passages to you. Your mind will be washed and renewed by the word until you have a more biblical outlook regarding money. If there are areas of your life that need to change, these will come into the light over a period of time, as the Holy Spirit convicts and gives grace to change. We all need to hear the truth over and over before it changes us, especially when a concept is new. Our spirits and unconscious minds grapple with the truth, and see if and how it applies; then, we are able to work it out in our own circumstances over time. It is rare that we can make a radical change the first time light shines on an area of our lives that needs it.

In short, for most of us, digging the well of provision requires time and some consistency. Others who are already walking in a great measure of faith and truth in this area may only need to read this book once to check for any small areas of new revelation.

In my own devotions, I periodically find that I need to reread the resources that helped me dig my wells initially. I query the Spirit (and try to access the weaknesses in my life) as to which topic needs to be read next, and rotate among several books. I look for new sources as well. I highly recommend *Your Promise of Protection* by Gloria Copeland for the well of protection and safety. We have enclosed a 14-day devotion that has changed my life greatly in the area of healing (see appendix 1).

The Lord may have already provided you with other books and resources designed to provide practical and/or scriptural advice regarding financial matters. Most of us need guidance in this area. However, once your mind has been significantly renewed and your well dug regarding faith for finances, you will be in a much better position to discern by the Spirit what advice is of the Lord and to put it into practice.

Let's get digging!

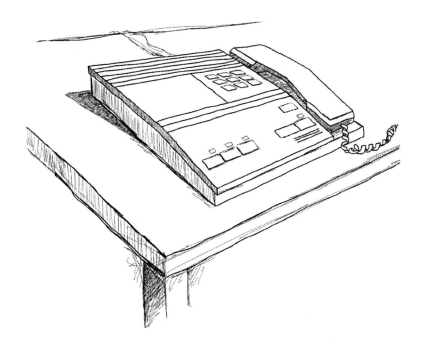

2.

PROVISION

As our savings evaporated, I kept praying for the Lord to provide for us. Whenever I prayed, I sensed that the Lord was saying not to worry, but to wait on Him. ("Don't keep asking—just trust Me.") I had hoped that the Lord would provide so we wouldn't need to delve into our retirement. It was a difficult day when we had to make the first large retirement withdrawal and pay the ten percent penalty in addition to the taxes on it. Still, the Lord seemed to be saying to wait on Him, that He had it under control. Then the time came when we made our last withdrawal, and all our resources were exhausted. Within a week, we took a trip with the worship team I was leading.

We went to a sister church in another state over a three-day weekend. As we traveled there, and again on the way back, I cried out to the Lord for help. This time, He didn't stop me, but I was able to pour out my heart to Him. I wasn't in self-pity, but was able verbalize our desperate need to Him. I also reminded Him of our giving and reminded Him of His promises to bless those who give to the poor, etc. There was no haughtiness now, only a cry to my heavenly Father for help.

When I reported to our tiny pathology lab on Monday, there was a voice message on the phone from Friday, the first day of our travel. A pathologist in a nearby city wondered if I might be able to do some temporary work for them. A colleague had become disabled and would be out for several months. I called, and he was willing to let me come home on weekends and early on Wednesdays so I could continue my responsibilities at my church. God had answered my prayer even while I was praying, and provided for us just when our need was greatest. Praise the Lord!

To enjoy the well of provision, we must have faith—faith to trust in God's sustaining power even when we do not have nearly enough, or when we have no income or resources at all. We must also believe that He wants to provide for us.

In His word, the Lord promises over and over again that He will never leave us or forsake us, and His promises include provision. Unless there is great, unrepentant sin in our lives, or we refuse to work, I believe that the Lord will provide our basic needs. When we repent and turn from our sin, the Lord will help us even when our financial need is the result of our own mistakes. His help does not mean that we won't be uncomfortable, or will not have to bear any consequences for our mistakes. His mercy is that we are not destroyed or trapped for life by our folly. He is merciful, and mindful that we are but dust. Our Father's very nature is to provide for us. He loves us so much that He gave . . . .

Prayer: *Lord, I believe that You are both able and willing to provide for me. You are my source of provision, not my job or the people in my life. Though You usually use those sources to provide for me, You are able and will provide when my job, friends and family all fail. I repent for the times when I have put my faith and trust in other sources of help instead of in You. Thank you for revealing my idolatry of trusting in work or savings, or other people before You. You are the God who provided for Your people in the desert with manna, meat, water, shade in the day, and fire by night. You are well able to meet my needs. Show me the part you want me to play in this process, for You said, "If a man will not work, he shall not eat." (I Thes. 3:10) I am willing to work hard, long and in humble circumstances as You desire. Help me to trust You. Teach me to have You as my greatest reward and not to just look for what You will give me. I want to seek Your Kingdom first, and I believe that as I do, You will provide the things I need. I ask these things in Jesus' name, Amen.*

Psalms 37:18-19: [18]The LORD knows the days of the blameless, and their inheritance will be forever. [19]They will not be ashamed in the time of evil, and in the days of famine they will have abundance. [3]

Psalms 37:23-28: [23]If the LORD delights in a man's way, he makes his steps firm; [24]though he stumble, he will not fall, for the LORD upholds him with his hand. [25]I was young and now I am old, yet I have never seen the righteous forsaken or their children begging bread. [26]They are always generous and lend freely; their children will be blessed. [27]Turn from evil and do good; then you will dwell in the land forever. [28]For the LORD loves the just and will not forsake his faithful ones. They will be protected forever, but the offspring of the wicked will be cut off. [1]

Prayer: *Lord, I am so grateful that You love me deeply and will never forsake me, though I am weak.*

Proverbs 10:2-3: [2]Ill-gotten treasures are of no value, but righteousness delivers from death. [3]The LORD does not let the righteous go hungry, but he thwarts the craving of the wicked.[1]

Matthew 6:24-34: [24]No one can serve two masters. Either he will hate the one and love the other, or he will be devoted to the one and despise the other. You cannot serve both God and Money. [25]Therefore I tell you, do not worry about your life, what you will eat or drink; or about your body, what you will wear. Is not life more important than food, and the body more important than clothes? [26]Look at the birds of the air; they do not sow or reap or store away in barns, and yet your heavenly Father feeds them. Are you not much more valuable than they? [27]Who of you by worrying can add a single hour to his life? [28]And why do you worry about clothes? See how the lilies of the field grow. They do not labor or spin. [29]Yet I tell you that not even Solomon in all his splendor was dressed like one of these. [30]If that is how God clothes the grass of the field, which is here today and tomorrow is thrown into the fire, will he not much more clothe you, O you of little faith? [31]So do not worry, saying, 'What shall we eat?' or 'What shall we drink?' or 'What shall we wear?' [32]For the pagans run after all these things, and your heavenly Father knows that you need them. [33]But seek first his kingdom and his righteousness, and all these things will be given to you as well. [34]Therefore do not worry about tomorrow, for tomorrow will worry about itself. Each day has enough trouble of its own. [1]

I Timothy 6:17-19: [17]Command those who are rich in this present world not to be arrogant nor to put their hope in wealth, which is so uncertain, but to put their hope in God, *who richly provides us with everything for our enjoyment.* [18]Command them to do good, to be rich in good deeds, and to be generous and willing to share. [19]In this way they will lay up treasure for themselves as a firm foundation for the coming age, so that they may take hold of the life that is truly life. [1]

Prayer: *Lord, thank you for providing so many things for my enjoyment. Create in me a generous heart. Where I feel like I don't have enough and have a stingy heart, convict me sorely. I don't want to cut off Your generous heart towards me.*

· · · · · · · · · · ·

The Testimony of Larry & Faithe

God's grace is so incredible; in fact, my vocabulary is inadequate to attempt to even describe just how marvelous God's love and mercy is. Jeremiah 29:11 is so very true, but at times it is difficult to see the overall plan God has for our lives. I suppose that if I have a favorite scripture it would have to be:

> **Lamentations 3:22-23:** 22 Through the Lord's mercies we are not consumed, because His compassions fail not. 23 They are new every morning; great is Your faithfulness. 2

It is enough to say that Faithe and I were severely injured emotionally from a church that we pastored in the late 80's-early 90's, where things went terribly wrong, and consequently I thought it best to take a sabbatical leave from pastoring. What I had intended to be months turned into six years. During that time God graciously allowed me to forgive and heal as we simply attended and received the word at a local church in Knoxville, Tennessee.

When that time was over, I accepted a position as pastor of a church in Michigan. Even though we were out of our comfort zone in the cold climate, we were very much at home with the people. They were just what we needed. They had been injured by a moral failure from their pastor, and were very much in need of healing also. We understood each other's needs perfectly. God is working even when we don't always perceive it!

Late one night in January, I was returning home from Grand Rapids and while traveling in the snowy conditions, my Aerostar went out of control on a bridge. As I veered off the highway and started down toward the river, all I had time to say was, "God have mercy on me!" The van was able to turn and avoid the river, and 45 minutes later someone came along and snaked me back up to the highway with their Jeep.

Obviously my vehicle was not well suited for the climate, so we began to pray and ask God to direct us to a 4x4 vehicle we could afford. We were pastoring in one of the poorest counties in Michigan and there were several weeks that we received no paycheck at all. But God is ever-faithful! I began to look online for vehicles and found a Jeep Grand Cherokee that I thought I could afford in a nearby town. Faithe did not have peace about the purchase, but I was full steam ahead. She continued to rein me in, saying, "God may have something much better than this Jeep for us."

We came in to see our family in Knoxville, and while attending the Sunday morning service at our old church, we were overwhelmed with the presence of God. At the close of the service, the pastor invited us to the stage. He related to the congregation that God's Spirit had spoken to him that morning to receive a special offering to help us purchase a suitable vehicle for Michigan weather. The next day at lunch, the pastor casually announced that my offering was $10,000. He said that I could either take the money and buy a vehicle, or I could take his one-year-old Expedition and owe $11,000. I chose to take over the Expedition, since it was much nicer and larger than what I could afford with the offering.

Just a few months later, Faithe and I were leading praise and worship at our church on a Sunday morning when the Holy Spirit interrupted us to say, "God is divinely can-celling debt in someone's life," and we continued with the worship service. The next day, the pastor from Knoxville called to say that a lady had come to him during his service and said she would like to give us $7,000. That was the exact amount that I needed to pay off the Expedition. I had no idea that God was divinely "cancelling debt" in our lives.

This is only one of many times God has divinely intervened in our lives. He is absolutely AWESOME!

3.

FUTILITY OF RICHES

One of the lies of the enemy is that wealth will bring joy and fulfillment, and will solve all of life's problems. Our problems are usually
due to our own faults and lack of character. Financial abundance
doesn't satisfy or fulfill the heart, and can easily fool us into believing or acting as though we don't need God. Poverty does bring great
stress and may create conflicts in relationships, but it also forces us
to see our great need for the Lord. I must seek Him for Himself, for
who He is. If I won't ask His will before making purchases and keep
myself aware of how desperately I need Him, then out of love for me,
He'll make sure I have to seek Him just to get my needs met.

Wealth creates its own stress. Money has to be managed. Loss of wealth produces great depression. Things need to be investigated, then purchased, then maintained and stored, all of which consumes our time and our affections. Unless I am fully committed, on guard and disciplined, these things will crowd out my time and therefore my affection for Him. I'll lose my first love.

Prayer: *Lord, help me to know that money is not the answer to my problems, but that You are what I really need. You know how much financial blessing I can handle and stay on fire for You. Don't give me more than I can handle, unless it is to test me for a short season. Teach me to be desperate for You, to love You more than all that money can buy. Show me how to stay humble no matter what my circumstances, so that You can finance Your kingdom through me as You desire. Teach me to adapt my lifestyle to Your will for me, not just to my current financial state. I want You to be able to trust me to pass on wealth, and not just enlarge my lust to spend everything I receive. In Jesus' name I ask it, Amen.*

Jeremiah 17:5-8: [5]Thus says the LORD, "Cursed is the man who trusts in mankind and makes flesh his strength, and whose heart turns away from the LORD. [6]For he will be like a bush in the desert and will not see when prosperity comes, but will live in stony wastes in the wilderness, a land of salt without inhabitant. [7]Blessed is the man who trusts in the LORD And whose trust is the LORD. [8]For he will be like a tree planted by the water, that extends its roots by a stream and will not fear when the heat comes; but its leaves will be green, and it will not be anxious in a year of drought nor cease to yield fruit."[3]

Job 15:31: [31]Let him not trust in emptiness, deceiving himself; for emptiness will be his reward.[3]

Job 30:15 [15]Terrors overwhelm me; my dignity is driven away as by the wind, and my prosperity has passed away like a cloud.[3/1]

Psalms 39:6-7: [6]Surely every man walks about like a shadow; surely they busy themselves in vain; He heaps up *riches,* and does not know who will gather them. [7]And now, Lord, what do I wait for? My hope *is* in You.[2]

Psalms 49:16-17: [16]Do not be overawed when a man grows rich, when the wealth *and* splendor of his house increases; [17]for he will take nothing with him when he dies, his wealth *and* splendor will not descend with him.[2/5]

Prayer: *Lord, help me not to be jealous of others, but to trust You for Your timing of blessing for my life. Deliver me from an ungrateful heart.*

Psalms 52:1a, 5-7: [1a]Why do you boast in evil, O mighty man? [5]But God will break you down forever; He will snatch you up and tear you away from *your* tent, and uproot you from the land of the living. *Selah.* [6]The righteous will see and fear, and will laugh at him, *saying,* [7]"Behold, the man who would not make God his refuge, but trusted in the abundance of his riches *and* was strong in his *evil* desire." [8]But as for me, I am like a green olive tree in the house of God; I trust in the loving kindness of God forever and ever. [3]

Prayer: *You are my refuge, Lord. I put my trust in You, for You alone can save, protect and truly bless me.*

Proverbs 11:4: [4]Riches do not profit in the day of wrath, but righteousness delivers from death.[3]

Proverbs 11:28: [28]He who trusts in his riches will fall, but the righteous will flourish like the *green* leaf.[3]

Ecclesiastes 5:15: [15]Naked a man comes from his mother's womb, and as he comes, so he departs. He takes nothing from his labor that he can carry in his hand. [1]

Isaiah 55:1-3: [1]Ho! Everyone who thirsts, come to the waters; and you who have no money come, buy and eat. Come, buy wine and milk without money and without cost. [2]Why do you spend money for what is not bread, and your wages for what does not satisfy? Listen carefully to Me, and eat what is good, and delight yourself in abundance. [3]Incline your ear and come to Me. Listen, that you may live; and I will make an everlasting covenant with you, *according to* the faithful mercies shown to David. [3]

Matthew 6:19-21: [19]Do not store up for yourselves treasures on earth, where moth and rust destroy, and where thieves break in and steal. [20]But store up for yourselves treasures in heaven, where moth and rust do not destroy, and where thieves do not break in and steal. [21]For where your treasure is, there your heart will be also. [1]

Matthew 13:22: [22]And the one on whom seed was sown among the thorns, this is the man who hears the word, and the worry of the world and the deceitfulness of wealth choke the word, and it becomes unfruitful. [3]

Matthew 16:26: [26]For what will it profit a man if he gains the whole world and forfeits his soul? Or what will a man give in exchange for his soul? [3]

John 12:24-25: [24]Truly, truly, I say to you, unless a grain of wheat falls into the earth and dies, it remains alone; but if it dies, it bears much fruit. [25]He who loves his life loses it, and he who hates his life in this world will keep it to life eternal. [3]

Prayer: *Holy Spirit, convict me of areas in my life that I've never yielded to You, the parts of the world and of my natural life to which I am very much alive. I want to be dead to the world and alive to You.*

I Timothy 6:17: [17]Command those who are rich in this present world not to be arrogant nor to put their hope in wealth, which is so uncertain, but to put their hope in God, who richly provides us with everything for our enjoyment. [18]Command them to do good, to be rich in good deeds, and to be generous and willing to share. [19]In this way they will lay up treasure for themselves as a firm foundation for the coming age, so that they may take hold of the life that is truly life. [1]

Prayer: *I humble myself before You, Lord. I hope in You, for only You can provide my real needs and bring fulfillment to my life. Teach me to give generously and lay up true treasures that will last.*

James 1:10-12: [10]But the one who is rich should take pride in his low position, because he will pass away like a wild flower. [11]For the sun rises with scorching heat and withers the plant; its blossom falls and its beauty is destroyed. In the same way, the rich man will fade away even while he goes about his business. [12]Blessed is the man who perseveres under trial, because when he has stood the test, he will receive the crown of life that God has promised to those who love him. [1]

4.

DILIGENCE

The Lord brought a wonderful Christian investment advisor into our lives and after meeting with him, we felt convicted that it was the time for us to begin to save for retirement. I calculated that I could be full-time in the ministry by age 52, if we put the maximum the government allowed, and also maxed out the previous year's retirement contribution by April 15. So we tightened our belts and postponed all major purchases and cut most of our other spending. We felt strapped during the catch-up phase (when we were saving two years' retirement in about 15 month), despite God's blessings on my business.

Just a few years later, when we had to draw the money out prematurely (because I was unemployed), the Lord worked a miracle. As we began to make withdrawals every month or two, the overall balance **before** each withdrawal was nearly what it was before the last one! The stock market was rising. I knew the Lord was sustaining us, and was honoring the diligence we had shown in saving. The Lord supported us for nearly two years with three years' of savings!

Adam was given work to do, and even in the paradise of Eden, he was to tend the Garden. After the fall, Adam came under a curse that he would produce from the ground with the sweat of his brow. Some argue that the curse was removed because of Christ's death for us. In any case, both the Old and New Testaments make it clear that we are to be good, diligent workers. We labor in the natural, and we labor in the spirit. Our labor in the spirit includes prayer, worship, evangelism, and ministering to the saints. Raising children as God intends falls into both categories. In whatever He has called us to, both natural and "spiritual", we are to do it with all our might and creativity, as unto Him. He has promised to reward us, as we look to Him.

Lord, I know that Your plan is for me to work with diligence, and that Your financial blessing usually comes through my labor. I look to You as my source, but that does not excuse laziness as I work unto You and in obedience to the people You have given authority over my life. I will work as You provide opportunity, and unless You direct otherwise. I know the finances are not just to benefit me, but are also so that I can be useful in financing Your kingdom. Help me to find the balance between hard, diligent work, and putting my trust in You to provide my needs. I pray these things and I honor You in the Name of Jesus. Amen!

2 Thessalonians 3:10: [10]For even when we were with you, we gave you this rule: "If a man will not work, he shall not eat." [1]

Proverbs 6:9-11: [9]How long will you lie there, you sluggard? When will you get up from your sleep? [10]A little sleep, a little slumber, a little folding of the hands to rest— [11]and poverty will come on you like a bandit and scarcity like an armed man...; [1]

Proverbs 10:4-5: [4]He who has a slack hand becomes poor, but the hand of the diligent makes rich. [5]He who gathers in summer *is* a wise son; he who sleeps in harvest *is* a son who causes shame. [2]

Proverbs 12:24, 27: [24]Diligent hands will rule, but laziness ends in slave labor. [27]The lazy man does not roast his game, but the diligent man prizes his possessions. [1]

I Corinthians 10:31: [31]Therefore, whether you eat or drink, or whatever you do, do all to the glory of God. [2]

Galatians 6:9: [9]Let us not become weary in doing good, for at the proper time we will reap a harvest if we do not give up. [1]

Proverbs 13:4: [4]The sluggard craves and gets nothing, but the desires of the diligent are fully satisfied. [1]

Proverbs 15:19: [19]The way of the sluggard is blocked with thorns, but the path of the upright is a highway. [1]

Proverbs 18:9: [9]He who is slothful in his work is a brother to him who is a great destroyer. [2]

Acts 20:33-35: [33]I have not coveted anyone's silver or gold or clothing. [34]You yourselves know that these hands of mine have supplied my own needs and the needs of my companions. [35]In everything I did, I showed you that by this kind of hard work we must help the weak, remembering the words the Lord Jesus himself said: 'It is more blessed to give than to receive.' [1]

Proverbs 19:15: [15]Laziness casts *one* into a deep sleep, and an idle person will suffer hunger. [2]

Proverbs 20:4, 13: [4]The sluggard does not plow after the autumn, so he begs during the harvest and has nothing. [3] [13]Do not love sleep or you will grow poor; stay awake and you will have food to spare. [1]

Proverbs 21:25-26: [25]The sluggard's craving will be the death of him, because his hands refuse to work. [26]All day long he craves for more, but the righteous give without sparing. [1]

Colossians 3:23: [23]Whatever you do, work at it with all your heart, as working for the Lord, not for men, [24]since you know that you will receive an inheritance from the Lord as a reward. It is the Lord Christ you are serving. [1]

Proverbs 22:3, 29: [3]A prudent man sees danger and takes refuge, but the simple keep going and suffer for it. [29]Do you see a man skilled in his work? He will serve before kings; he will not serve before obscure men. [1]

Proverbs 24:30-34: [30]I went past the field of the sluggard, past the vineyard of the man who lacks judgment; [31]thorns had come up everywhere, the ground was covered with weeds, and the stone wall was in ruins. [32]I applied my heart to what I observed and learned a lesson from what I saw: [33]A little sleep, a little slumber, a little folding of the hands to rest—[34]and poverty will come on you like a bandit and scarcity like an armed man. [1]

Proverbs 27:18: [18]He who tends a fig tree will eat its fruit, and he who looks after his master will be honored. [1]

Proverbs 28:19, 20: [19]He who works his land will have abundant food, but the one who chases fantasies will have his fill of poverty. [20]A faithful man will be richly blessed, but one eager to get rich will not go unpunished. [1]

Ecclesiastes 11:6: [6]Sow your seed in the morning and do not be idle in the evening, for you do not know whether morning or evening sowing will succeed, or whether both of them alike will be good. [3]

Luke 12:42-44: [42]And the Lord said, "Who then is that faithful and wise steward, whom *his* master will make ruler over his household, to give *them their* portion of food in due season? [43]Blessed *is* that servant whom his master will find so doing when he comes. [44]Truly, I say to you that he will make him ruler over all that he has." [2]

Proverbs 27:23-24: [23]Be diligent to know the state of your flocks, *and* attend to your herds; [24]for riches do not endure forever, and a crown is not secure for all generations.

I Peter 4:11: [11]If anyone speaks, he should do it as one speaking the very words of God. If anyone serves, he should do it with the strength God provides, so that in all things God may be praised through Jesus Christ. To him be the glory and the power for ever and ever. Amen. [1]

. . . .

MARSHA'S TESTIMONY -
PART ONE

I had been invited to a meeting to hear a missionary from Africa. I've always been drawn to missionaries no matter where they serve. Having spent some time in Africa (Kenya & Tanzania), I was interested to hear what this missionary fellow had to say. He was from southern Africa, and many of the small villages were coming to Christ. The problem was there were not nearly enough Bibles for these new Christians. I thought about my Bible and how much the Word of God means to me. I could not survive without its instruction and comfort. My heart was touched.

I had come planning to give an offering, and I had already "figured out" how much I could give. As I heard the need, I said, "Lord, I want to do more, but I only have so much to give." I prayed, "Father, what do you want me to give?"

"Give $100," I heard Him say. Of course I'm going to obey the Lord, but my flesh started to reason with me in the following internal conversation.

"I only have $101 in the bank, and I have bills coming due that need to be paid. I don't having a paying job – what will I do if I give that? Shut up, flesh; the worst that can happen is that I don't have the money for the bills. I have to trust Father to meet them anyway." I wrote out the check for $100 and placed it in the offering plate as it went by.

My flesh screamed at me, "What have you done? It's not too late. Chase down the usher and get the check back. Tell him you made a mistake." Once again, I told my flesh to be quiet; it will be all right.

After the service I got in my car (which the Lord had GIVEN us) and turned on my cell phone, which I had turned off during the meeting. I had a voice mail. The message was from a friend telling me she had an offering for my ministry, AND she had some things she needed done that she would pay me to do. The Lord had provided for me before I had even given the offering. When it was all said and done, I had more than double what I had given in that offering. What an awesome God!

5.

GIVING

During the years we spent at our church in Georgia, the Lord taught and convicted us greatly about our giving. We sowed into the church, into missions, into the benevolence ministry of the church and however we felt the Lord's leading. The Lord worked on my heart to be generous in little things like picking up the tab for others when we ate with them. We had extra people living with us who needed to be fed.

As our finances dried up, we had to drop back tremendously in our giving. We noticed that our friends began spontaneously treating us when we went out to eat. Things got most serious a few months after the five-month temporary job finished. The Lord, by this time, had called me into the ministry and I knew I would be leaving at some point to start a church. But there was still a mortgage and utilities to pay and mouths to feed. For about six months, we stayed one month away from bankruptcy. The Lord provided from the most unexpected sources. My mentally handicapped nephew heard we were in need and told his dad that since he was rich, he wanted to give us $200 from his savings! A close brother in the church felt compelled by the Lord to give me a whole week's paycheck. The small church we were in banded together and painted our house for us so we could sell it. Then they gave us a generous offering to enable us to move, when the time came. Each month the Lord worked a miracle to enable us to pay our obligations. Once I couldn't make the whole mortgage, but when I called, they let me use a one-time emergency plan and I didn't have to pay the escrow. The next month, He provided the whole amount.

God built our faith during those six months. He showed us that we were reaping from the giving we had been doing. He let us know that as He had required us to learn to give, now we had to learn to receive. (The former is more fun!) God is good, and cannot be out-given.

Giving includes gifts of our time, physical belongings and money. Financial giving begins *after* the tithe, with offerings and alms. (We "pay" or owe the first tenth to God, and shouldn't designate it, except to our local church or our pastor.) After our tithe, the Lord wants us to give under the leading of His Spirit, out of hearts that are longing to give. Normally when the opportunity presents itself, we should be asking how much to give, not whether to give. Not giving should be an unusual occurrence, requiring confirmation. It is also possible, however, to give excessively, out of emotion or religious tradition, rather than because the Spirit is prompting us.

God gives us seed for sowing and bread for eating (II Cor. 9:10). The bread is what we eat and pay our bills with. The seed is what we sow into God's Kingdom to reap a harvest of God's provision during the next season. Both seed for sowing and grain for bread come from the same wallet or bank account, and only the Lord can show us which is which. Obedience is the key. There are seasons for radical giving and seasons when we are in such need that giving is meager, though no less a sacrifice (times for receiving). Whenever I find myself frequently resisting thoughts that I should give generously (when needs are presented), I know I'm in trouble and need to get radical in my giving. Fortunately, my wife usually has a more generous heart than I, and can usually hear the Lord when I can't. I've learned to listen to her, especially when a spirit of poverty seems to have gripped my heart.

Lord, I know You are most often hindered in Your blessing of my life by the smallness in my heart to give to You and to others. Make me a radical, prompt-to-do-it, cheerful, big-hearted giver. Help me remember that as I give with the right motives, You will provide seed for more giving, and will provide for my needs. Grant me wisdom in my giving and help me to hear Your voice clearly. Forgive the stinginess in my heart, and remind me of how You and others have given so generously to me. In Your great name I ask it, Amen.

II Corinthians 9:6-15: 6Now this *I say,* he who sows sparingly will also reap sparingly, and he who sows bountifully will also reap bountifully. 7Each one *must do* just as he has purposed in his heart, not grudgingly or under compulsion, for God loves a cheerful giver. 8And God is able to make all grace abound to you, so that always having all sufficiency in everything, you may have an abundance for every good deed; 9as it is written,

"HE SCATTERED ABROAD, HE GAVE TO THE POOR,

HIS RIGHTEOUSNESS ENDURES FOREVER."

10Now He who supplies seed to the sower and bread for food will supply and multiply your seed for sowing and increase the harvest of your righteousness; 11you will be enriched in everything for all liberality, which through us is producing thanksgiving to God. 12For the ministry of this service is not only fully supplying the needs of the saints, but is also overflowing through many thanksgivings to God.3

Lord Jesus, I want to be able to give abundantly to every good work as Your Spirit leads. Help me to sow liberally according to the little

I have now, so I'll have an abundance to give as my harvest comes in.

Proverbs 3:9-10: [9]Honor the LORD from your wealth and from the first of all your produce; [10]so your barns will be filled with plenty and your vats will overflow with new wine. [1]

I Chronicles 29:2: [2]Now for the house of my God, I have prepared with all my might: gold for *things to be made of* gold, silver for *things of* silver, bronze for *things of* bronze, iron for *things of* iron, wood for *things of* wood, onyx stones, *stones* to be set, glistening stones of various colors, all kinds of precious stones, and marble slabs in abundance. [3]Moreover, because I have set my affection on the house of my God, I have given to the house of my God, over and above all that I have prepared for the holy house, my own special treasure of gold and silver [5] ... for all kinds of work *to be done* by the hands of craftsmen. Who *then* is willing to consecrate himself this day to the LORD? [2]

Ezra 2:69: [69]According to their ability they gave to the treasury for the work 61,000 gold drachmas and 5,000 silver minas and 100 priestly garments.[1]

Proverbs 11:24-25: [24]One man gives freely, yet gains even more; another withholds unduly, but comes to poverty. [25]A generous man will prosper; he who refreshes others will himself be refreshed. [1]

Ecclesiastes 5:13-15: [13]There is a grievous evil *which* I have seen under the sun: riches being hoarded by their owner to his hurt. [14]When those riches were lost through a bad investment and he had fathered a son, then there was nothing to support him. [15]As he had come naked from his mother's womb, so will he return as he came. He will take nothing from the fruit of his labor that he can carry in his hand. [3]

Ecclesiastes 11:1, 2: [1]Cast your bread upon the waters, for you will find it after many days. [2]Give a serving to seven, and also to eight, for you do not know what evil will be on the earth. [3]

Matthew 6:19-21: [19]Do not store up for yourselves treasures on earth, where moth and rust destroy, and where thieves break in and steal. [20]But store up for yourselves treasures in heaven, where moth and rust do not destroy, and where thieves do not break in and steal. [21]For where your treasure is, there your heart will be also.[1]

I Corinthians 16:1-2: [1]Now about the collection for God's people: Do what I told the Galatian churches to do. [2]On the first day of every week, each one of you should set aside a sum of money in keeping with his income, saving it up, so that when I come no collections will have to be made. [1]

II Corinthians 8:1-4: [1]And now, brothers, we want you to know about the grace that God has given the Macedonian churches. [2]Out of the most severe trial, their overflowing joy and their extreme poverty welled up in rich generosity. [3]For I testify that they gave as much as they were able, and even beyond their ability. Entirely on their own, [4]they urgently pleaded with us for the privilege of sharing in this service to the saints. [1]

II Corinthians 8:9: [9]For you know the grace of our Lord Jesus Christ, that though He was rich, yet for your sakes He became poor, that you through His poverty might become rich. [2]

II Corinthians 8:11-15: [11]Now finish the work, so that your eager willingness to do it may be matched by your completion of it, according to your means. [12]For if the willingness is there, the gift is acceptable according to what one has, not according to what he does not have. [13]Our desire is not that others might be relieved while you are hard pressed, but that there might be equality. [14]At the present time your plenty will supply what they need, so that in turn their plenty will supply what you need. Then there will be equality, [15]as it is written: "He who gathered much did not have too much, and he who gathered little did not have too little." [1]

Galatians 6:6: [6]Anyone who receives instruction in the word must share all good things with his instructor. [1]

Philippians 4:15-19: [15]Now you Philippians know also that in the beginning of the gospel, when I departed from Macedonia, no church shared with me concerning giving and receiving but you only. [16]For even in Thessalonica you sent *aid* once and again for my necessities. [17]Not that I seek the gift, but I seek the fruit that abounds to your account. [18]Indeed I have all and abound. I am full, having received from Epaphroditus the things *sent* from you, a sweet-smelling aroma, an acceptable sacrifice, well pleasing to God. [19]And my God shall supply all your need according to His riches in glory by Christ Jesus. [2]

· · · · · · · · · · ·

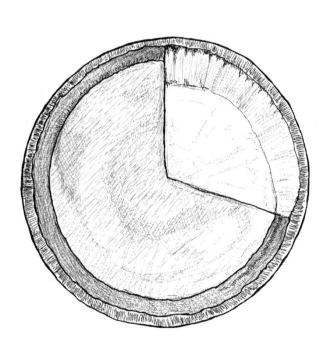

Linda's Testimony (Part 1)

In 1993, I had been in a test for five years. The enemy of my soul was going for the knockout, but God had a different idea about the whole ordeal. These testings involved five major areas in my life. They were as follows:

1) My stepson was shot in a road rage incident and pro-nounced dead on arrival; 2) My other son, David, backslid because of the death of his brother; 3) David married an unbeliever; 4) My mother, who was a dear friend to me, died; and 5) My husband of eighteen years asked for a divorce.

In the midst of these testings, God's voice was loud and clear to me. He told me that for the next five years He wanted me to give one third of my gross income to Him as an offering (in addition to my tithe). I promised Him that I would. It was May of 1993, and I had just left my job at a mercantile store, a place of safety with wonderful benefits. (I had six weeks' paid vacation, three hundred and ninety-five accumulated sick days, health insurance, and a 401k plan.) I left to start a business by renting a station in a free-standing hair styling salon and becoming my own boss. Little did I know that my security was going to be found only "in the Lord." I had no benefits, no insur-ance, and no pay if I did not work. My hours were cut to three days a week and I suddenly went to having no hus-band to back me up (in what I had promised the Lord).

What a test of my faith! Oh, but how miraculously our Lord and Savior works! He came through and for five years I kept my oath to the Lord, and never went without. I never wanted for one thing! I saw the Lord move in ways I had never expected. He kept up my health. He supplied all my needs. All strings of security had to be torn from me to allow Him to prove Himself to me.

I have been single now for fifteen years and stand in amazement of how my husband in the Lord has done (and continues to do) all He said He would do. I still work three days a week, am buying my home, drive a new car and most importantly, give tithes and offerings off the top. To God be the glory!

6.

LOVE OF MONEY

While we believed the Lord was going to be sending me out to a new job and to pastor a church, we did not know *when*. The Lord had also indicated on more than one occasion that He was going to bless our finances. I was really praying in earnest and believing God for a major miracle, all the while also believing in God for our mortgage, etc.

One day, during my devotions, the words of a song pierced my heart. The singer threw in an extra phrase and said to the Lord, "You're my great reward." Almost immediately I felt the Spirit impress me that He was not my great reward, but that the financial blessing from Him that I was seeking, was the "great reward" I really wanted. I was horrified—pierced to the core, and immediately repented and asked for forgiveness. I told the Lord that He was my greatest reward. I stopped praying at all about the financial promises, and every time the thought of them would come up, I thrust those thoughts aside and focused instead on the joy of knowing Him. I must have said, "Lord, You're my great reward," a hundred times or more.

Two weeks later I received a call (a voice message) from a pathologist asking if I was still looking for a job. He had a position open and said that He was a fellow believer in Jesus Christ. We interviewed one week later and had a signed contract for the job in another week. I firmly believe that the last thing the Lord had to do in my heart in that season was to remove the *root* of the love of money that had crept in at a terribly deep level. By His grace I was able to repent, and then He was able to bless us.

If riches increase, do not set *your* heart *on them.* (Psalms 62:10 [2]) While money itself is not evil, the Bible refers to the love of it as "the root of all evil". Most of us have strong desires at times for increase in finances, or for possessions we don't have, but want. The simple desires are not evil, *if* we yield the desires to Him, and they cause us to seek Him. If my seeking Him is for what *He* wants for me, then it is pure. If, however, my prayers are focused only on what I want, or I want those things I'm praying for more than I desire Him, then I've slipped into the love of money (into idolatry). I've begun to worship the created thing more than the Creator.

If my desires have any real grip on me, they must die. Only what is laid on God's altar can be resurrected to life. God will usually require that a cherished dream be released to Him and laid on the altar, so that my intense desires die. Do I love Him more, or the thing I want? I must give my dream to Him as an offering. It then becomes His, not mine.

Abraham had to release his desire for a son while he waited on God to fulfill His promise. As a result, He received a son, Isaac. Much later, at God's command, he had to place Isaac on an altar to sacrifice him to the Lord. So too, I may have to give up my desires several times. Then God can bless me with the thing I once craved, because I will be a steward, and the possession will not possess me.

A good test of whether my desires are respectable in God's eyes is how I respond when God asks me to give it away. When He requires the money that I have saved for a cherished dream, or prompts me to give away more than I had planned or budgeted, how do I respond? If I can yield willingly to Him, I'm probably free from the love of money. We must remain passionate and vigilant about not allowing things to possess us. Remember that we serve a jealous God. Many people can stay zealous for God and pursue Him through times of great need. As my friend, Dr. Benny Hand, Sr. says, only a very few believers can stay true to their first love of Him and keep pursuing Him in long seasons of abundance.

*Lord, I choose to have no other gods before You. I want to be free from the love of money. I desire and need Your blessing. Please help me learn to be only a steward of the things You allow me to have. I want to use or give them away however and whenever You desire, and for Your glory. Expose any hidden pockets of greed or selfishness in my heart. Help me turn **from** my selfishness **to** You, and to be free from the wrongful love of money. Make my heart desperate for You without having to be driven to desperation by poverty and need. Make me a conduit for Your blessing to others. Show me where You can't trust me to be a steward. Send people into my life as I need them, to reveal my wicked ways and to help me change. I pray these things knowing that You will answer, in Jesus Christ's name, Amen.*

I Samuel 2:7-10: [7]The LORD sends poverty and wealth; he humbles and he exalts. [8]He raises the poor from the dust and lifts the needy from the ash heap; he seats them with princes and has them inherit a throne of honor. For the foundations of the earth are the LORD'S; upon them he has set the world. [9]He will guard the feet of his saints, but the wicked will be silenced in darkness. It is not by strength that one prevails; [10]those who oppose the LORD will be shattered. He will thunder against them from heaven; the LORD will judge the ends of the earth. He will give strength to his king and exalt the horn of his anointed. [1]

Ecclesiastes 5:10-12: [10]He who loves money will not be satisfied with money, nor he who loves abundance *with its* income. This too is vanity. [11]When good things increase, those who consume them increase. So what is the advantage to their owners except to look on? [12]The sleep of the working man is pleasant, whether he eats little or much; but the full stomach of the rich man does not allow him to sleep.[3]

Matthew 6:24: [24]No one can serve two masters; for either he will hate the one and love the other, or he will be devoted to one and despise the other. You cannot serve God and wealth.[3]
Lord, I commit to serve You alone.

Mark 10:21-27: [21]Looking at him, Jesus felt a love for him and said to him, "One thing you lack: go and sell all you possess and give to the poor, and you will have treasure in heaven; and come, follow Me." [22]But at these words he was saddened, and he went away grieving, for he was one who owned much property.

[23]And Jesus, looking around, said to His disciples, "How hard it will be for those who are wealthy to enter the kingdom of God!" [24]The disciples were amazed at His words. But Jesus answered again and said to them, "Children, how hard it is to enter the kingdom of God! [25]It is easier for a camel to go through the eye of a needle than for a rich man to enter the kingdom of God." [26]They were even more astonished and said to Him, "Then who can be saved?" [27]Looking at them, Jesus said, "With people it is impossible, but not with God; for all things are possible with God."[3]

Haggai 1:4-9: [4]"Is it a time for you yourselves to be living in your paneled houses, while this house remains a ruin?" [5]Now this is what the LORD Almighty says: "Give careful thought to your ways. [6]You have planted much, but have harvested little. You eat, but never have enough. You drink, but never have your fill. You put on clothes, but are not warm. You earn wages, only to put them in a purse with holes in it." [7]This is what the LORD Almighty says: "Give careful thought to your ways. [8]Go up into the mountains and bring down timber and build my house, so that I may take pleasure in it and be honored," says the LORD. [9]"You expected much, but see, it turned out to be little. What you brought home, I blew away. Why?" declares the LORD

Almighty. "Because of my house, which remains a ruin, while each of you is busy with his own house." [1]

Luke 9:25: [25]What good is it for a man to gain the whole world, and yet lose or forfeit his very self?[1]

Job 22:24-25: [22:24]And place *your* gold in the dust, and *the gold of* Ophir among the stones of the brooks, [25]Then the Almighty will be your gold and choice silver to you.[3]

I Timothy 6:9-11: [9]But those who desire to be rich fall into temptation and a snare, and *into* many foolish and harmful lusts which drown men in destruction and perdition. [10]For the love of money is a root of all *kinds of* evil, for which some have strayed from the faith in their greediness, and pierced themselves through with many sorrows. [11]But you, O man of God, flee these things and pursue righteousness, godliness, faith, love, patience, gentleness. [2]
Yes, Holy Spirit, show me how I need to flee, to run away from greed and the love of money.

II Timothy 3:1-5: [1]But mark this: There will be terrible times in the last days. [2]People will be lovers of themselves, ***lovers of money***, boastful, proud, abusive, disobedient to their parents, ***ungrateful***, unholy, [3]without love, unforgiving, slanderous, without self-control, brutal, not lovers of the good, [4]treacherous, rash, conceited, ***lovers of pleasure rather than lovers of God***—[5]having a form of godliness but denying its power. ***Have nothing to do with them.*** [1]
Lord, help me to stay away from the influence of those who worship self, pleasure and the "good life". Show me how to decrease the effect that the secular press and media is having on my heart, and strengthen me against it. I repent for taking on the standard of the world.

. . . .

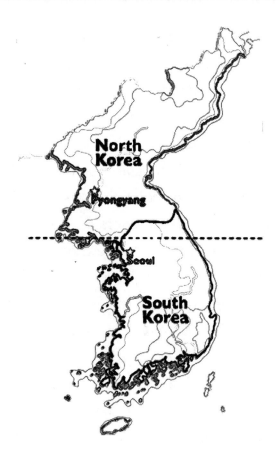

MARSHA'S TESTIMONY – PART TWO

My life has been one of trusting God for every need, and Father has been more than faithful; He has been SO good. I've been a tither since I received my first dime. My mother instilled in me the principle of tithing at a very early age. I loved to give to God and still do. We didn't have abundance as a large family, but because my mother was a tither, we always had food on the table, clothes to wear, and a place to call home. We were a very religious family. My mother and grandmother imparted to me a deep love for God, but I had a lot to learn about His deep, abiding love for me and His desire to bless me.

My first mission trip came right after I graduated college in 1974. I was going to South Korea for six weeks with a group from different parts of the U.S. Although I had graduated, I had to complete a genetics course at a local university that summer. I was working the night shift at a nursing home, and was also doing odd jobs trying to raise the funds for the trip. I worked hard, but was paid little.

That summer I was the song leader and missions speaker for VBS. The previous summer I had helped raise funds for some missionaries going to Hong Kong and China. I had told the kids if they raised a certain amount in the offering by the end of the week, I would let them throw water balloons at me. Well, the adults got involved then, and we raised the amount and some more besides.

This time I was the mission's speaker. I did a repeat performance with the water balloons. A week or so before I was to have my ticket and travel expenses sent in, I still didn't have nearly enough. I left VBS, heading to work. I was so tired and discouraged. I pulled off to the side of the road and cried out to God, pouring out my heart to Him, and then went on to work. VBS ended. Just before the deadline for the funds to be turned in, a man from the church came to me and asked me how much I still needed for the trip. He wrote a check for the balance of the trip and told me if I needed anything else to let him know; he would take care of it. He had planned to pay for the whole mission trip, but was waiting so that others would have an opportunity to give.

Father God had it covered the whole time while I was struggling, fretting and working myself to a frazzle. It's taken a long time, but I am learning more and more to rest in Him and ALL His promises. My part is to trust Him and His integrity, and to do whatever He tells me to do.

7.

FAITH IN THE POWER
OF GOD TO SUSTAIN

One evening, my wife Martha and I were eating out with our pastor and his wife. He told us of an opportunity to go to Israel with others from a Bible college with which we were involved. This was many years before I became the pathology director. The trip sounded wonderful, but was very expensive. The church was small and couldn't afford to send anybody overseas. Martha, however, grabbed hold of the idea and was sure the trip was of the Lord, and that He would provide. We began saving, but ever so slowly, and it seemed preposterous. Every time our pastor (or I) questioned

Martha about it, she said that she *knew* that the Lord would do it. None of the other three of us had faith in it, but she had enough for all of us. Little by little, and up until the last minute, the Lord provided, and we had a glorious trip that has changed our lives ever since. I have no doubt, however, that if Martha had not both had and kept that faith strong, we would have never seen the inside of an airplane going towards the Middle East.

Faith to trust God for finances *can* be difficult. Some of us were taught that prayer about finances was somehow dirty, or an unworthy subject for us to bring before the Lord. That idea, however, is not biblical. We know that our Lord Jesus Christ spoke about finances all the time, and about our attitudes towards them. God wants us to know that He is concerned about every area of our lives, and wants our dependence to be on Him. He desires for us to ask Him about our financial concerns. We are to ask for everything we need and request His guidance about how we should use the things He entrusts to us. As we ask Him, God will lead us and provide for us. He will work in our hearts to build a wonderful relationship with Him, and provide faith to trust Him for all our needs.

Dear Lord, forgive me for when I've not trusted You to provide for my needs, and also for when I've not asked You how I should use my possessions. I do put my trust in You. I acknowledge that You are not limited by my resources, and have no trouble providing for everything that is in Your will for me. Help me to hear Your voice so I will have the confidence to believe You with unshakeable faith. Let my faith for Your provision bring joy to Your heart as I trust You like a little child. I love You, Lord. You are so good! I ask these things in the name of Jesus Christ, my Lord. Amen.

Matthew 10:29-31: 29Are not two sparrows sold for a cent? And *yet* not one of them will fall to the ground apart from your Father. 30But the very hairs of your head are all numbered. 31So do not fear; you are more valuable than many sparrows. *3*

Psalms 34:8-10: 8Oh, taste and see that the LORD *is* good; Blessed *is* the man *who* trusts in Him! 9Oh, fear the LORD, you His saints! *There is* no want to those who fear Him. 10 The young lions lack and

suffer hunger; but those who seek the LORD shall not lack any good *thing.* ²
Yes Lord, I do trust in You and also reverence You. I believe that as I trust You, I'll not lack one good thing. I trust You to know what's best for me.

Deuteronomy 8:3: ³So He humbled you, allowed you to hunger, and fed you with manna which you did not know nor did your fathers know, that He might make you know that man shall not live by bread alone; but man lives by every *word* that proceeds from the mouth of the LORD. *²*

Psalms 32:10: ¹⁰ Many are the sorrows of the wicked, but he who trusts in the LORD, loving kindness shall surround him.*³*
Thank you Father for Your loving kindnesses to me!

Matthew 21:21-22: ²¹And Jesus answered and said to them, "Truly I say to you, if you have faith and do not doubt, you will not only do what was done to the fig tree, but even if you say to this mountain, 'Be taken up and cast into the sea,' it will happen. ²²"And all things you ask in prayer, believing, you will receive." *³*

Psalms 37:4-5: ⁴Delight yourself also in the LORD, and He shall give you the desires of your heart. ⁵Commit your way to the LORD, trust also in Him, and He shall bring *it* to pass. *²*

Psalms 52:8-9: ⁸But I am like an olive tree flourishing in the house of God; I trust in God's unfailing love for ever and ever. ⁹I will praise you forever for what you have done; in your name I will hope, for your name is good. I will praise you in the presence of your saints. *¹*

Proverbs 3:5-6: ⁵Trust in the LORD with all your heart, and lean not on your own understanding; ⁶In all your ways acknowledge Him, and He shall direct your paths. *²*

John 14:12-14: ¹²Truly, truly, I say to you, he who believes in Me, the works that I do, he will do also; and greater *works* than these he will do, because I go to the Father. ¹³Whatever you ask in My name, that will I do, so that the Father may be glorified in the Son. [14]If you ask Me anything in My name, I will do *it*. [3]

Lord, show me Your will, and Your timing. I want to pray and receive all the things You have for me and for others around me, in Your perfect timing.

Lamentations 3:21-24: [21]This I recall to my mind, therefore I have hope. [22]The LORD'S loving kindnesses indeed never cease, for His compassions never fail. [23]*They* are new every morning; great is Your faithfulness. [24]"The LORD is my portion," says my soul. "Therefore I have hope in Him."[3]

Mark 11:24: [24]Therefore I say to you, all things for which you pray and ask, believe that you have received them, and they will be *granted* you. [3]

I John 4:18: [18]There is no fear in love. But perfect love drives out fear, because fear has to do with punishment. The one who fears is not made perfect in love.[1]

Lord, I know I cannot walk in fear and faith at the same time. So I choose to believe that You saw my situation coming long ago, and that You have it under control. I believe that Your love for me is an active love, and that You will accomplish the greatest glory for Yourself and greatest good for me out of this situation, as I keep my eyes on You. In Jesus' name I pray!

Philippians 4:6-7: [6]Do not be anxious about anything, but in everything, by prayer and petition, with thanksgiving, present your requests to God. [7]And the peace of God, which transcends all understanding, will guard your hearts and your minds in Christ Jesus.[1]

John 14:27: [27]Peace I leave with you; my peace I give you. I do not give to you as the world gives. Do not let your hearts be troubled and do not be afraid.[1]

Isaiah 41:12-13: [12] Though you search for your enemies, you will not find them. Those who wage war against you will be as nothing at all. [13]For I am the LORD, your God, who takes hold of your right hand and says to you, "Do not fear; I will help you."[1]

I Peter 1:7: [7]These have come so that your faith—of greater worth than gold, which perishes even though refined by fire—may be proved genuine and may result in praise, glory and honor when Jesus Christ is revealed.[1]

I Peter 5:7: [7]...casting all your anxiety on Him, because He cares for you. [3]

· · · · · · · · · · ·

Pastor Benny Hand's Testimony

My wife, Nelda, and I were into our third year as "faith" missionaries to Nicaragua. By the word faith, I mean we had no income other than what was generated each month from the hearts of the individuals and churches who saw fit to donate to our ministry. We had assumed the responsibility of supplying the complete physical needs of 15 individuals – four in our family and eleven natives. Our finances were a close call each month. One Christmas we spent less than $3.00 on our own children.

For almost two years we had not written a single check from our account in the States that was not in the red. It took 15 days for a check written in Nicaragua to arrive to our bank account in the States. There was always enough each month donated by various sources and deposited by our home church into our bank account that by the time the "faith" checks arrived they were all covered. A bad check written in Nicaragua was a definite prison sentence and sometimes without a trial. I once knew of a man in Guatemala who wrote a bad check for $800.00. He was arrested on one day and was serving a two-year prison sentence beginning the next day. The bad check negated any wasted time and money spent on a trial. The check was evidence enough. Nicaragua's laws were very similar. Each month we were taking a big chance, but we had no other options.

Once a month we received, by mail, a financial report from our home church of donations received and deposited into our bank account in the States. We would also receive our bank statement telling us of our written checks and their deposits. Every month for almost two years the church report total had sufficed the bank statement's deficit. Our own daily records never recorded a check written that was in the black. Every check we wrote was a faith check. Then one month things took a down turn. When we received the two reports it showed, for the first time, there was not going to be enough to cover the checks. Before the next month's deposit would be made, we would be $450.00 short and our last few checks would bounce. We had no way to cover the checks. The two reports spoke loudly that I was going to jail. Nelda and I cried out to the Lord as to what to do. We received a common and simple plan of action: fast and pray for three days, and believe for a miracle. We had time to do this before the checks would arrive in the States and then be returned by the bank to Nicaragua.

We agreed to fast and pray for the three days and not go to the mailbox during that time. We usually went to the mailbox daily, because it was our connection to our finances, relatives and friends. I told Nelda that I heard the Lord say the resolution to our dilemma would arrive at the end of the third day. It seemed most likely that the mailbox would be the carrier of good news by faith.

We completed the three-day fast and it was time to go check the mail. I rode my motorcycle to the post office praying in the Spirit and with much anticipation that God would come through for us. Sure enough, there was an air mail letter from the States. It was from someone who had never written to me before. He was a pastor I had casually met only one time previously and I expected to never see again. In his letter he wrote, "I was traveling from Columbus, Ga. to LaGrange, Ga. and the Lord spoke to me and told me to go and put $500.00 in your account. It is done..."

Unbelievably, God provided a miracle by speaking to a casual acquaintance in another country and made provision for His own. I knew without a doubt that God loved me!

8.

TITHING AND FIRST FRUITS

Tithing is a concept that we, at least in America, have tended to look at as just another part of giving. Because some have doubted that New Testament believers even need to tithe, we have spent most of our efforts in this area deciding *whether* to tithe or not. The study of learning *how* to tithe, i.e., what are the principles whereby we can learn to be excellent in our tithing, has often been neglected. We believe that biblical tithing is foundational for the believer who desires to be in a position to receive God's full provision for his life.

While tithing is a concept that is considered in the New Testament (see below, Heb. 7:1-2), it is primarily developed in the Old

Covenant, in the law of Moses. It preceded the law, however, and both Abraham and Jacob tithed (10%). The comparison of New Testament (or New Covenant) tithing with that in the law is complicated, because their tithe was twenty percent, and every third year it was thirty percent, with the additional ten percent going to the poor and the Levites. We can learn a great deal concerning the principles of tithing by looking at Abraham's practice of tithing *before* the law was given, and at the "first fruits" part of giving/tithing *under* the law. In these examples, the money or "increase" was given to someone else (someone "greater"). Also, in the law, it was not up to the giver to decide who should receive his tithe or first fruit. In the case of the first fruits, it went to the priests and Levites, and in Abraham's case, to Melchizedek. In both cases, the giving was "off the top"; it took place *before* the giver consumed any part of the increase. Abraham didn't go through the loot and take what he wanted first, before tithing. The first fruits of the harvest and the first male offspring were the Lord's and the first fruits were given *before* the remainder of the harvest could be touched.

We believe that the pattern in the word (as sketched above) mandates that the tithe (10% of all increase) belongs to the local body of Christ (or more accurately to leadership of the local church). Needs such as "temple or tabernacle" building and repair should ideally come from offerings, over and above the tithe.

The first fruits were devoted to God, and the word devoted (Heb. *harem* or *charem*—Strongs 2764) means "devoted to destruction or devoted wholly to God." Common or personal use was forbidden. The clearest example is of the city of Jericho. It was the first city taken in the Promised Land, and as such was a first fruits of their conquest and was devoted wholly to the Lord (Joshua 6 & 7). It was to be burned with fire. The gold and silver were the Lord's and were to be brought into His treasury. Achan, however, took some gold, silver and articles of clothing from Jericho for himself. The Lord's blessing and protection departed from Israel, and in their next battle they fled before the inhabitants of Ai. Thirty-six men died. When Joshua sought the Lord, He said,

"Israel has sinned; they have violated my covenant, which I commanded them to keep. They have taken some of the devoted things (Heb. - harem); they have stolen, they have lied, they have put them with their own possessions. ¹²That is why the Israelites cannot stand against their enemies; they turn their backs and run, because they have been made liable to destruction (Heb. – harem). I will not be with you anymore unless you destroy whatever among you is devoted to destruction (harem)." (Joshua 7:11-12)[1]

We believe that the tithe is the Lord's; it doesn't belong to us. We don't **"give"** the tithe, because it is not *ours* to give, but is the Lord's. In a sense, we **"pay"** the tithe. We pay someone what is rightfully theirs (we *pay* our electric bills.) We do not specify what it is to be used for, because it is not ours to direct. (We don't dictate to the electric company that they use our payment only for new construction!) The tithe must leave our control and go to the Lord. The offering, on the other hand, is over and above the tithe, and is given voluntarily and can be designated. In a sense, the tithe is seed sown for our most basic needs; food, clothing and shelter (and to rebuke the devourer). Offerings are seed sown for other blessings and desires that we may have.

It is obvious in the example of Jericho, and from Malachi 3 (quoted below), that tithing is also important in blocking the enemy from stealing from us. Tithing **and** offering open the windows of heaven for God's blessing. Of all the truths presented in this devotion, we consider tithing to be one of the most important, and it is foundational to the other principles in the area of provision.

Many people we know and have heard of began to tithe when they really could not afford to at all. Their budget was already stretched to the max! Yet, in faith as they began to tithe, they were amazed to see God move to stretch their finances or provide sovereignly to meet their needs. The testimony of Lyn and her unsaved husband (which is coming at the end of this section) is an example. Just as unsaved Cornelius' alms went up to God (Acts 10) and God sent Peter to him so that Cornelius and his household were saved, so God responded to this family's tithing and worked a miracle.

Lord, I ask You to forgive me for where I have failed to tithe, when I've not given the tithe first, or when I've used Your tithe to support my own ministry or ministries of my choosing. Please remind me, Holy Spirit, of when I've overlooked income sources and not tithed on them, or given only a partial "tithe". I repent to You. I choose to give You the tithe as Your word says; FIRST, and without a complaining heart. As I tithe, please also show me what I should give you as an offering, for all I have is Yours. I believe You know my needs and will meet them, for You (and not my job or checkbook) are my Source. According to Your word, since I am tithing and bringing offerings, I ask You to rebuke the devourer for my sake. I ask You to open the windows of heaven (of blessing) in my life and for those around me. Let it be for Your glory. Please put the fear of God on me in this area so that I will never rob You again. In Jesus' name I pray, Amen!

Malachi 3:7-12: "[7]Ever since the time of your forefathers you have turned away from my decrees and have not kept them. Return to me, and I will return to you," says the LORD Almighty. "But you ask, 'How are we to return?' [8]Will a man rob God? Yet you rob me. But you ask, 'How do we rob you?'
In tithes and offerings. [9]You are under a curse—the whole nation of you—because you are robbing me. [10]Bring the whole tithe into the storehouse, that there may be food in my house. Test me in this," says the LORD Almighty, "and see if I will not throw open the floodgates of heaven and pour out so much blessing that you will not have room enough for it. [11]I will prevent pests from devouring your crops, and the vines in your fields will not cast their fruit," says the LORD Almighty. "[12]Then all the nations will call you blessed, for yours will be a delightful land," says the LORD Almighty. [1]

Genesis 14:18-20: [18]Then Melchizedek king of Salem brought out bread and wine. He was priest of God Most High, [19]and he blessed Abram, saying, "Blessed be Abram by God Most High, Creator of heaven and earth. [20]And blessed be God Most High, who delivered your enemies into your hand."
Then Abram gave him a tenth of everything. [1]

Hebrews 7:1-2a: [1]This Melchizedek was king of Salem and priest of God Most High. He met Abraham returning from the defeat of the kings and blessed him, [2]and Abraham gave him a tenth of everything. [1]

Matthew 23:23: [23]Woe to you, teachers of the law and Pharisees, you hypocrites! You give a tenth of your spices—mint, dill and cumin. But you have neglected the more important matters of the law—justice, mercy and faithfulness. You should have practiced the latter, *without* neglecting the former. [1] (italics mine)

Genesis 28:20-22: [20]Then Jacob made a vow, saying, "If God will be with me and will watch over me on this journey I am taking and will give me food to eat and clothes to wear [21]so that I return safely to my father's house, then the LORD will be my God [22]and this stone that I have set up as a pillar will be God's house, and of all that you give me I will give you a tenth." [1]

Ezekiel 44:30: [30]The first of all the first fruits of every kind and every contribution of every kind, from all your contributions, shall be for the priests; you shall also give to the priest the first of your dough to cause a blessing to rest on your house. [3]

Exodus 22:29-30: [29]You shall not delay *to offer* the first of your ripe produce and your juices. The firstborn of your sons you shall give to Me. [30]Likewise you shall do with your oxen *and* your sheep. It shall be with its mother seven days; on the eighth day you shall give it to Me. [2]

Exodus 34:19-20: [19]All that open the womb *are* Mine, and every male firstborn among your livestock, *whether* ox or sheep. [20]But the firstborn of a donkey you shall redeem with a lamb. And if you will not redeem *him,* then you shall break his neck. All the firstborn of your sons you shall redeem.
And none shall appear before Me empty-handed. [2]

Exodus 34:26a: [26]Bring the best of the first fruits of your soil to the house of the LORD your God. [1]

Leviticus 23:9-10: [9]And the LORD spoke to Moses, saying, [10]"Speak to the children of Israel, and say to them: 'When you come into the land which I give to you, and reap its harvest, then you shall bring a sheaf of the first fruits of your harvest to the priest.'" [2]

Leviticus 27:30: [30]A tithe of everything from the land, whether grain from the soil or fruit from the trees, belongs to the LORD; it is holy to the LORD. [1]

Numbers 3:13: [13]". . . for all the firstborn are mine. When I struck down all the firstborn in Egypt, I set apart for myself every firstborn in Israel, whether man or animal. They are to be mine. I am the LORD." [1]

Numbers 18:25-32: [25]The LORD said to Moses, [26]"Speak to the Levites and say to them: 'When you receive from the Israelites the tithe I give you as your inheritance, you must present a tenth of that tithe as the LORD'S offering. [27]Your offering will be reckoned to you as grain from the threshing floor or juice from the winepress. [28]In this way you also will present an offering to the LORD from all the tithes you receive from the Israelites. From these tithes you must give the LORD'S portion to Aaron the priest. [29]You must present as the LORD'S portion the best and holiest part of everything given to you.'
[30]Say to the Levites: 'When you present the best part, it will be reckoned to you as the product of the threshing floor or the winepress. [31]You and your households may eat the rest of it anywhere, for it is your wages for your work at the Tent of Meeting. [32]By presenting the best part of it you will not be guilty in this matter; then you will not defile the holy offerings of the Israelites, and you will not die.'" [1]

Deuteronomy 18:4-8: [4]You are to give them [*the priests*] the first fruits of your grain, new wine and oil, and the first wool from the shearing of your sheep, [5]for the LORD your God has chosen them and their descendants out of all your tribes to stand and minister in the LORD'S name always. [6]If a Levite moves from one of your towns anywhere in Israel where he is living, and comes in all earnestness to the place the LORD will choose, [7]he may minister in the name of the LORD his God like all his fellow Levites who serve there in the presence of the LORD. [8]He is to share equally in their benefits, even though he has received money from the sale of family possessions. [1] (*Tithing does not depend on the need or lack of need of the leadership receiving it.*)

Deuteronomy 26:10-11: [10]' . . . and now, behold, I have brought the first fruits of the land which you, O LORD, have given me.' Then you shall set it before the LORD your God, and worship before the LORD your God. [2]

Nehemiah 10:35-39: [35]We also assume responsibility for bringing to the house of the LORD each year the first fruits of our crops and of every fruit tree. [36]As it is also written in the Law, we will bring the firstborn of our sons and of our cattle, of our herds and of our flocks to the house of our God, to the priests ministering there. [37]Moreover, we will bring to the storerooms of the house of our God, to the priests, the first of our ground meal, of our grain offerings, of the fruit of all our trees and of our new wine and oil. And we will bring a tithe of our crops to the Levites, for it is the Levites who collect the tithes in all the towns where we work. [38]A priest descended from Aaron is to accompany the Levites when they receive the tithes, and the Levites are to bring a tenth of the tithes up to the house of our God, to the storerooms of the treasury. [39]The people of Israel, including the Levites, are to bring their contributions of grain, new wine and oil to the storerooms where the articles for the sanctuary are kept and where the ministering priests, the gatekeepers and the singers stay. We will not neglect the house of our God. [1]

. . . .

THE TESTIMONY OF LYN (Part 1)

In the summer of 1993, my church had a visiting minister who spoke about finances. My husband was not a Christian at this time. I had recently quit my well-paying job as a partner at a CPA firm to start my own business. My husband's business, building and installing custom cabinets, was not doing well. He had plenty of work, but no profit. (He had been a successful drummer years before, but had quit.) Since I was just starting my business, I was not making much money either. This meant I did not have much money to give to my church, which troubled me. I had approached my husband once before about tithing and offering from his money, knowing the principals of God's word, but he just looked at me like I was crazy and said, "I don't think so."

When this visiting minister began preaching on finances, I felt an urging by the Holy Spirit to approach my husband again regarding giving to the church. He said, "If it will make things better, do it. You just handle it." Then I had to figure out how to "tithe" or offer, since we usually showed a loss on the business. I felt like God gave me a plan and I began giving from my husband's business.

In December of that same year our church hosted a week-long meeting with an outside speaker. My pastor felt compelled by the Lord to ask my unsaved husband to play the drums with the band. During the conference, my husband was awesomely born again and baptized with the Holy Spirit (see that story later in Part 2). I know that, like Cornelius in Acts 10, he started sowing for his own salvation when he began giving to the church. Today he is the senior pastor of the same church to which he first began giving. He is truly a changed man.

Our finances didn't change overnight, but with counsel from our pastor and God, the business turned around to make a profit and paying our bills is not a worry any more. The Lord worked several other miracles along the way. In fact, we have more than enough, so we get to give even more!

9.

STEWARDSHIP

One of the lies in our self-absorbed western culture is that our stuff belongs to us. Part of our covenant with the Lord, however, is that we belong to Him. This includes everything we have and are. We give Him ourselves, our possessions, our past (including our sins), and our future. He, in turn, gives us Himself and everything He has and is (as we mature and can handle it in a godly way). Since everything I have is the Lord's, I am only a steward of the things that He entrusts to me, not an owner. I can use the stuff, but not possess it. There is great freedom in having use of something without owning it. It can never possess me, since it can be required of me at any time. I have greater responsibility to take care of the things I "have" since they belong to another, and I must give an account of them to Him when He asks it of me. The great danger in forgetting that I am only a steward is that I become guilty of taking ownership of what is not mine; something we usually call stealing. I wonder what kind of blessing or curse I could expect to receive upon "my" possessions in that case!

At one point in our lives, we were looking for a house to buy for our family. We were expecting to bring an Ethiopian man from his country to live with us and attend college (and we were not finished adding more children to our family), so we needed quite a few bedrooms. We looked at every four or more bedroom house in the town anywhere close to our price range, and could find nothing that seemed right for us. We had decided to buy land and build, but our land deal fell through.

Martha found an ad in the newspaper for a house on sale by a bank. It was in foreclosure. She went and saw it, and then called me. The house was not only just what we were looking for, but much, much more. The Lord guided us in what to offer and how high to go, but the bank would not sell it. I clearly felt like I was supposed to release the house back to the Lord (put the house on "the altar"), walk away from it and forget about it, which I did. I really felt like we would not be buying it. Four weeks later, while on the way back from vacation, I had the distinct sense from the Lord that I was supposed to go to the bank president and talk to him about the house. I did, and the next day they met the terms the Lord had given us and we had a signed contract. It cost about half what it would have cost to build a large, modest house, but the house was absolutely grand and was built on 4½ acres in the city, with a big circular driveway. There were fancy things in the house that I had never even heard of.

During the time when we were considering the house, Martha struggled with the house because it was ostentatious to us. We wanted a house that looked modest on the outside (but was big on the inside). The Lord rebuked her (for her pride), and said if He wanted to bless us with a grand house, we were to receive it with thankfulness and without complaining. Then He revealed a truth to her. When the Lord blesses us, we are to receive the blessing with thankfulness, but

FROM ZERO TO HERO IN YOUR FINANCES

to hold the blessing loosely. That way the house would be His, and we would to be ready to give it back to Him at any time.

Over a year before, when He called us to move to this area, we had left our new "dream" house (after owning it only a year), to obey Him. He let me know that because we had obeyed, that He had blessed us (1½ years later) with a house *beyond* my dreams. He also revealed to us (in the natural and by the Spirit) that this house was an example of the wealth of the sinner being stored up for the righteous. (Prov. 13:22).

Lord, I repent for acting as though the things You have entrusted to me are my own. I realize I've unwittingly stolen them from You, and so now I give ownership of everything in my care back to You. Though I'm not worthy to be a steward anymore, I ask You by Your grace to allow me to continue on as a steward of the things You've entrusted to me. Help me to take proper care of them and remember whose they are. Anything in my custody that you want at any time, feel free to use in any way You desire or to transfer it to another person. Thank you for the use of all these things. I give myself to You afresh, and trust myself to Your care. I freely acknowledge that mine is the better part of the covenant we have with each other. I gladly exchange all my riches, failures and sins for who You are, Your blessing on my life, and Your riches. I pray these things in Jesus' wonderful name, Amen.

Matthew 25:14-30: [14]Again, it will be like a man going on a journey, who called his servants and entrusted his property to them. [15]To one he gave five talents of money, to another two talents, and to another one talent, each according to his ability. Then he went on his journey. [16]The man who had received the five talents went at once and put his money to work and gained five more. [17]So also, the one with the two talents gained two more. [18]But the man who had received the one talent went off, dug a hole in the ground and hid his master's money. [19]After a long time the master of those servants returned and settled accounts with them. [20]The man who had received the five talents brought the other five. 'Master,' he said, 'you entrusted me with five talents. See, I have gained five more.'
[21]His master replied, 'Well done, good and faithful servant! You have

been faithful with a few things; I will put you in charge of many things. Come and share your master's happiness!'

22The man with the two talents also came. 'Master,' he said, 'you entrusted me with two talents; see, I have gained two more.'

23His master replied, 'Well done, good and faithful servant! You have been faithful with a few things; I will put you in charge of many things. Come and share your master's happiness!'

24Then the man who had received the one talent came. 'Master,' he said, 'I knew that you are a hard man, harvesting where you have not sown and gathering where you have not scattered seed. 25So I was afraid and went out and hid your talent in the ground. See, here is what belongs to you.'

26His master replied, 'You wicked, lazy servant! So you knew that I harvest where I have not sown and gather where I have not scattered seed? 27Well then, you should have put my money on deposit with the bankers, so that when I returned I would have received it back with interest.

28'Take the talent from him and give it to the one who has the ten talents. 29For everyone who has will be given more, and he will have an abundance. Whoever does not have, even what he has will be taken from him. 30And throw that worthless servant outside, into the darkness, where there will be weeping and gnashing of teeth.' 2

Lord Jesus, I want to be like one of the first two servants who invested your money wisely and made a profit for You. I'll need Your help to succeed, and ask You for it. I love You!

I Corinthians 4:2b: . . . it is required of stewards that one be found trustworthy.3
Holy Spirit, please expose to me any areas where I've been untrustworthy so I can ask forgiveness and change my ways.

Matthew 25:44-46: 44They also will answer, 'Lord, when did we see you hungry or thirsty or a stranger or needing clothes or sick or in prison, and did not help you?' 45He will reply, 'I tell you the truth, whatever you did not do for one of the least of these, you did not do for me.' 46Then they will go away to eternal punishment, but the righteous to eternal life. 1

Matthew 6:19-21, 24, 33: [19]Do not store up for yourselves treasures on earth, where moth and rust destroy, and where thieves break in and steal. [20]But store up for yourselves treasures in heaven, where neither moth nor rust destroys, and where thieves do not break in or steal; [21]for where your treasure is, there your heart will be also.[24]No one can serve two masters; for either he will hate the one and love the other, or he will be devoted to one and despise the other. You cannot serve God and wealth. [33]But seek first His kingdom and His righteousness, and all these things will be added to you. [3]

Luke 16:9-13: [10]Whoever can be trusted with very little can also be trusted with much, and whoever is dishonest with very little will also be dishonest with much. [11]So if you have not been trustworthy in handling worldly wealth, who will trust you with true riches? [12]And if you have not been trustworthy with someone else's property, who will give you property of your own? [1]

[13]No servant can serve two masters; for either he will hate the one and love the other, or else he will hold to one and despise the other. You cannot serve God and mammon. [3]

I Timothy 5:8: [8]If anyone does not provide for his relatives, and especially for his immediate family, he has denied the faith and is worse than an unbeliever. [1]

I Timothy 6:17-19: [17]Command those who are rich in this present world not to be arrogant nor to put their hope in wealth, which is so uncertain, but to put their hope in God, who richly provides us with everything for our enjoyment. [18]Command them to do good, to be rich in good deeds, and to be generous and willing to share. [19]In this way they will lay up treasure for themselves as a firm foundation for the coming age, so that they may take hold of the life that is truly life. [1]

• • • • • • • • • •

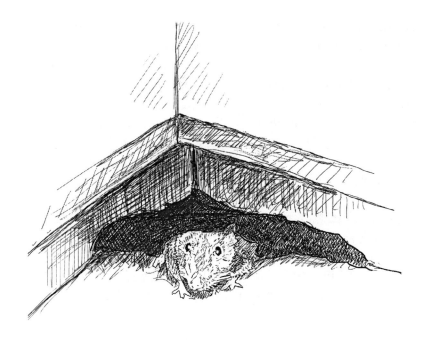

THE TESTIMONY OF LYN (Part 2)

When we first got married, my husband and I lived in the house he grew up in. We lived there for about 18 years. He and his brothers and sister remained the owners of the property, so we didn't want to put too much money into the place. It was old and really needed more repair than it was prudent to perform. We struggled with the leaky roof, many holes for rats and roaches to use to invade my home, sagging floors, etc. I really wanted a new home, but we were struggling just to pay our bills.

Since I became a Christian in 1988, I have been faithful to give my tithes and offerings. God began working on my character and required me to be content – not complaining about my house, but being thankful that I had a place to live. He also required that I take care of it as best I could with the money we had. I came to the place where I was willing to live in our home until I died – and to the natural mind that seemed to be exactly what would happen.

In 2000, my dad told me that he wanted to give my husband and me $80,000. Now this was the dad who did not approve of my marriage (an inter-racial marriage), and had met my husband only a few years prior to this, after *many* years of our marriage. I was shocked. This meant we would be able to buy or build a new home! It hadn't happened overnight, but because of my being faithful to God's principal of giving, and allowing God to mold my character and develop contentment in me, He blessed us abundantly. We now live in a beautiful home which should be completely paid for in about 10 years (or less if that's what God wants).

10.

SOWING AND REAPING

The law of sowing and reaping is so significant in this context that it needs its own section. Probably everything in God's creation is based on it. We know that in nature, plants and animals reproduce after their own kind, with increase (multiplication). We do not always recognize, however, that everything we do, good or bad, is also a sowing to the flesh or to the spirit, and reaps a harvest after its own kind, always with increase. It often takes a while to reap, usually months and sometimes years, but God and His word are not mocked (see Gal 6:7-9 below). The financial aspect of sowing and reaping is only one of many applications, but will be emphasized here. By the way, if you want the Lord and others to be merciful to you (you want them to see your heart, not just your actions), then sow mercy to others.

In spiritual sowing and reaping, we must think like farmers. One of the obstacles and potential deceptions to be overcome may develop when a person radically changes either for the good or bad. For a season he is still reaping the harvest from the previous seed he planted. The recently backslidden person often decides that all the teaching about God blessing the righteous is a bunch of bunk, because his life is still going along just fine. He doesn't realize that he is living on the harvest from the good seed sown before. It may take many months before the old harvest wears out and the new one kicks in when he will reap the error of his ways, to his great sorrow. On the other hand, the newly saved or newly tithing person wonders why things seem to stay so hard for him. Even though he is giving more, he is still reaping a harvest of lack from his past when he was robbing God; a tough combination. If he is faithful for a season, however, the new harvest of blessing will kick in, and the old harvest will begin to give out. God does give grace, however, and sometimes allows reaping from the newfound obedience to be unusually fast, particularly for young believers.

One word on II Corinthians 9:6-15, below, which is all about giving. Notice in verse ten, Paul talks about God supplying *seed for sowing* and *bread for food*. We see that financial provision is made to enable us to give or sow into His Kingdom, as well as to supply our various needs (including that of saving). According to this passage, God supplies both; only we have to discern which is which.

Two obvious points arise from this simple truth. First, if we are giving obediently, we can ask for more seed to sow and scripturally expect the Lord to answer. Secondly, we can err in eating/consuming our seed (bad news for a farmer) or err by sowing what God intended for "bread" to meet our needs and the needs of our family. The latter usually arises from giving (out of compulsion or a false sense of duty) what God intended to meet our needs. So we must discern what to sow (give) and what to eat by the Spirit. He will show us through the word and with the wisdom God has given either to us or to others in our lives (especially our spouses). By such discernment we will know what to give and what to keep, because it is "bread" for our family, not "seed" to be sown.

One day, I realized how blessed we were financially and asked the Lord why He put me in medicine. I went to medical school because of a very clear leading (a word) from the Lord (confirmed three times). Though I didn't do it for money at all, the Lord has blessed me greatly through the profession. As I pondered the question with thankfulness, He reminded me of an experience I had in first grade. I was in a Lutheran school while my parents were in seminary, preparing to go to the mission field. The school was preparing to take up an offering for a special project. All the kids were encouraged to save up their money for the day of the special offering, which would be taken up during a chapel service. My parents were struggling seminary students themselves and I had no allowance or other income. I had, however, been given $5 as a present from a relative. I felt convicted by the Lord to give the $5 for the offering. I became sick with the measles shortly before the special chapel service, so I wrote a simple note to go with the $5 and asked my dad to give the money to the school. My dad gave the money with the note to the school principal and told him it represented all I owned. The principal was somehow greatly encouraged by the story, and read the note and told the story to the entire student body at the time of the offering.

What I felt impressed with by the Holy Spirit, some 35 years later, was that the small offering I had given was a seed. The harvest that He chose for me to reap was my going into medicine. Although He usually does things for more than one reason, I now know one reason why. (Be very careful when you are tempted to prevent your kids from radical giving. You could be cutting off their blessing.)

Lord, I desire to sow for a harvest of righteousness by doing good deeds as You lead by Your Spirit, and by giving "seed" that You provide. I ask You to provide "seed" for me to sow where I am lacking. Help me to know by Your Spirit what, in my wallet and bank account, is "seed" and what is "bread". Help me to be obedient to give the seed. I believe that as I do, You will give me a harvest so that I will have more seed to sow. I ask these things for Your honor and glory, for the strengthening of Your Kingdom, and so that thanksgiving and

*praise will arise to Your name because of the seed sown. In Jesus'
name I pray. Amen.*

II Corinthians 9:6-15: ⁶Remember this: Whoever sows sparingly
will also reap sparingly, and whoever sows generously will also reap
generously. ⁷Each man should give what he has decided in his heart
to give, not reluctantly or under compulsion, for God loves a cheerful giver. ⁸And God is able to make all grace abound to you, so that
in all things at all times, having all that you need, you will abound in
every good work. ⁹As it is written:
    "He has scattered abroad his gifts to the poor;
    his righteousness endures forever."
**¹⁰Now he who supplies seed to the sower and bread for food will
also supply and increase your store of seed and will enlarge the
harvest of your righteousness.** ¹¹You will be made rich in every way
so that you can be generous on every occasion, and through us your
generosity will result in thanksgiving to God.
¹²This service that you perform is not only supplying the needs of
God's people, but is also overflowing in many expressions of thanks
to God. ¹³Because of the service by which you have proved yourselves, men will praise God for the obedience that accompanies your
confession of the gospel of Christ, and for your generosity in sharing
with them and with everyone else. ¹⁴And in their prayers for you their
hearts will go out to you, because of the surpassing grace God has
given you. ¹⁵Thanks be to God for his indescribable gift! ¹

Galatians 6:6-10: ⁶The one who is taught the word is to share all
good things with the one who teaches *him*. **⁷Do not be deceived,
God is not mocked; for whatever a man sows, this he will also
reap.** ⁸For the one who sows to his own flesh will from the flesh reap
corruption, but the one who sows to the Spirit will from the Spirit
reap eternal life. ⁹Let us not lose heart in doing good, for *in due time*
we will reap if we do not grow weary. ¹⁰So then, while we have
opportunity, let us do good to all people, and especially to those who
are of the household of the faith. ³ (*Bold and italics mine*)

Psalms 126:4-6: ⁴Turn to freedom our captivity *and* restore our for-
tunes, O Lord, as the streams in the South [are restored by the tor-
rents]. ⁵They who sow in tears shall reap in joy *and* singing. ⁶He who

goes forth bearing seed and weeps [at needing his precious supply of grain for sowing], shall doubtless come again with rejoicing, bringing his sheaves with him. 5

Lord, when I feel poor after radical giving, help me to hang on in faith while I wait on You. Help me to really trust, though I'm weeping inside, that You are a rewarder of those that seek and obey You. Open my eyes to Your blessings on my life.

Proverbs 11:17-19: 17The merciful man does good for his own soul, but *he who is* cruel troubles his own flesh. 18The wicked *man* does deceptive work, but he who sows righteousness *will have* a sure reward. 19As righteousness *leads* to life, so he who pursues evil *pursues it* to his own death. 2

Proverbs 11:24, 25: 24One man gives freely, yet gains even more; another withholds unduly, but comes to poverty. 25A generous man will prosper; he who refreshes others will himself be refreshed. 1

Proverbs 11:27,30, 31: 27He who diligently seeks good seeks favor, but he who seeks evil, evil will come to him. 30The fruit of the righteous is a tree of life, and he who is wise wins souls. 31If the righteous will be rewarded in the earth, how much more the wicked and the sinner! 3

Ecclesiastes 11:1, 2: 1Cast your bread upon the waters, for you will find it after many days. 3

Hosea 8:7: 7For they sow the wind and they reap the whirlwind. The standing grain has no heads; it yields no grain. Should it yield, strangers would swallow it up. 3

Hosea 10:11-12a: 12Sow for yourselves righteousness, reap the fruit of unfailing love, and break up your unplowed ground; for it is time to seek the LORD, until he comes and showers righteousness on you. 13But you have planted wickedness, you have reaped evil, you have eaten the fruit of deception. 1

Acts 10:1-4,44-48a: 1At Caesarea there was a man named Cornelius, a centurion in what was known as the Italian Regiment. 2He and all his family were devout and God-fearing; he gave generously to those in need and prayed to God regularly. ³One day at about three in the afternoon he had a vision. He distinctly saw an angel of God, who came to him and said, "Cornelius!"⁴ Cornelius stared at him in fear. "What is it, Lord?" he asked. The angel answered, "Your prayers and gifts to the poor have come up as a memorial offering before God. . ." ¹

· · · · · · · · · · ·

THE TESTIMONY OF LYN (PART 3)

In December of 1993, my church had a camp meeting with Pastor Dale Brooks. We rented a conference room at a local hotel and invited everyone. Our praise and worship leader, John, was looking for musicians to join with him during the meetings. My husband is a drummer (he had played professionally with James Brown, Percy Sledge, and Otis Redding), but was not a Christian at that time. My pastor, Mack Ballard, believed that only Christians should minister on a praise and worship team. However, God shook up his theology and told him to ask my husband, A.T., to play with the team. So, John asked me to ask my husband if he would play the drums for this camp meeting. When I asked him, he said he didn't have time to do that. Well, I did not deliver the message, supposing my husband and John would talk.

One evening we invited John and his family to have dinner with us. While there, John mentioned that all the musicians that had committed to playing at the camp meeting had canceled. Now, I must preface this next part with the fact that my husband has always had a very merciful heart. John looked him in the eyes and said, "You're still coming, aren't you?"

My husband, who thought I had delivered the message that he could not make the camp meeting, felt much compassion for John, knowing how it feels to be disappointed, and simply said, "I'll be there." Even though there was much grumbling and complaining to me afterwards, I knew he would keep his word.

When it came time for the meeting, my husband, our granddaughter (whom we were raising) and I rode together since we had only one vehicle. The meetings started on Sunday night and lasted through Friday. Pastor Brooks had prophesied over me the Sunday night prior to the camp meeting that the thing I had desired and been praying for was about to come to pass. I knew he was talking about my husband's salvation, but saw no movement from my husband toward God.

Monday night came and went, and the meeting was wonderful, but my husband seemed to be untouched by what was happening. Tuesday and Wednesday nights were repeats of Monday night.

My mother came to our home on Thursday so she could go to the meetings with us. My husband is a very hard worker and I, feeling much compassion for him, told him we would ride to the meeting with my mom and he could come separately so he could leave after praise and worship if he wanted to. He was very excited to hear that, but I cautioned him that he should talk with John before he left to make sure it was okay to leave early. He talked with John, who said, "You know Pastor Ballard. He might call us back up to play at any time." My husband was disappointed, but resigned himself to the fact that he would have to stay the entire night.

Another piece of the puzzle that God was putting together had to do with my husband's daughter, Vette. She (not a Christian at this time) came to the meeting on Thursday night and sat behind my husband and myself. Pastor Brooks wanted everyone who worked at Central State Hospital to come up so he could pray for them and that was where Vette worked. She did not go up for prayer, so I turned to encourage her to go up and even offered to go up with her, but she smiled and said no. At that time, God spoke to my husband and said, "Your daughter is the spitting image of you; she doesn't know Me and doesn't want to know Me because you don't know Me." He later said that it was as if God had held up a mirror to his face as He spoke. My husband didn't hear anything else that was said after that because he was so full of shame. When the pastor gave the altar call, my husband went forward and surrendered to God through the blood of Jesus Christ. What a wonderful journey it has been and continues to be!

This story always amazes me, because of all the circumstances God worked out to bring my husband to that moment where he could hear Him speak. Our God is worthy of our awe.

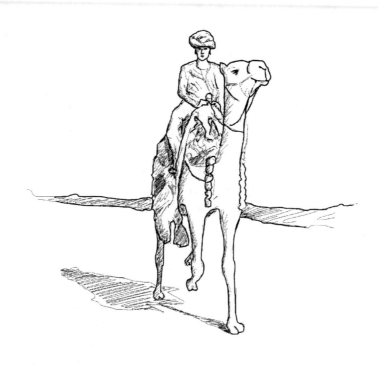

11.

PROSPERITY

The "rich young ruler" was told by Jesus that if he wanted to be perfect to "go, sell your possessions and give to the poor, and you will have treasure in heaven. Then come, follow me (Matt. 19:21)." The man went away sadly "because he had great wealth."

Jesus' disciples were amazed. Jesus said to them, "I tell you the truth, it is hard for a rich man to enter the Kingdom of heaven." I always thought the scripture was talking only about salvation and eternal life, but I think there is a deeper truth. Two words need fuller definitions.

The "Kingdom of God" has been equated with heaven/eternal life, but in scripture the term is usually talking about this life. "The Kingdom of God is not a matter of eating and drinking, but of righteousness, peace and joy in the Holy Spirit, because anyone who serves Christ in this way is pleasing to God and approved by men (Romans 14:17-18)." Clearly, the context is of this life. Jesus consistently equated the coming of the Kingdom with healing the sick, casting out demons, and raising the dead. When God's Kingdom comes, the King has His way and things happen! Perhaps the Kingdom of God is best "defined" by Jesus' prayer as that in which God's will is done on earth as it is in heaven. (No sick, demon oppressed or dead there!)

The second word to be further defined is 'rich' (not at all the same as prosperous by our definition). The young man is said to have had great wealth. I think, functionally, being rich in this manner can be defined by the following: A person of "great wealth" no longer *feels* the need for faith in God for finances. He (or she) can make most purchasing decisions without regard to money, not because of great faith, but because of great natural abundance. Also, in the case of this man, he could not give up his wealth for the Lord (idolatry by definition). Prosperity, by contrast, implies the lack of debt, having basic needs met, and (primarily) the ability to give whenever the opportunity arises and as the Holy Spirit leads. All these may be done by faith, and do not imply large amounts of monetary reserves. ("Large monetary reserves" result in a natural (not faith based) freedom from any financial concerns.)

Many of us have desired more so we would no longer need to seek the Lord and use faith in the financial realm. Yet, without faith it is impossible to please God. We need to repent of these motivations. God wants to be our source, instead of our treasure being our source. I believe there is a great danger in amassing great wealth. There are few who can walk in the fullness of the Kingdom (loving and pursuing the Lord with all their mind, heart, soul and strength) and possess riches. We are right to walk in a sober fear of the Lord regarding significant wealth. How tragic to lose our first love, and our destinies in God, for possessions down here.

The Lord's desire, however, has always been to *prosper* His people. His promises of prosperity, both to Israel and in the new covenant, are always conditional. He knows that financial/physical prosperity without prosperity of character will ruin us, and He wants His best for us. He is a lavish giver, and loves to bless His children. Although the enemy would have us think He is stingy and gives begrudgingly, just the opposite is true. If, however, our faith and expectation is for God to be stingy, then we will block much of the good He desires for us. Hebrews 11:6 says, "⁶And without faith it is impossible to please God, because anyone who comes to him must believe that he exists and that he rewards those who earnestly seek him." ¹So we must believe that if we seek Him, He will reward us. (Read Job to see how God put a hedge about him. After Job was tested and found faithful, God blessed Job with twice as much as before.)

During medical school I had an opportunity to travel overseas to do a two-month training rotation. There was an opening at a mission hospital in Zaire (the Congo) that looked perfect. The trip took place a few weeks after my wife and I were married. Neither of us had any finances for such an endeavor, but we prayed. A Methodist church in town gave us $500 through the school. Then, by a series of miracles, my parents, missionaries to Tanzania, were enabled to help us with the rest of the expense. The trip was really a honeymoon for us. We got to spend a couple of days in Athens, Greece. The Lord even arranged for us to fly business class across the Atlantic! The entire trip was wonderful, yet we were "poor" students. Our heavenly Father, however, is not poor and gave us a wonderful wedding present in each other and in the "honeymoon." He is so good.

Lord, I thank You that You are a good God and want to prosper me in every way. You know what I need most and when I need it. You know what things I can handle and what would cause me to grow lukewarm towards You. I trust You to bless me greatly, beyond my wildest dreams, and to also keep me on fire for you. I know that You are looking for reasons to bless me, like a natural father looks for excuses to get things for his kids. I believe that as I seek You, and line up with Your word, that You will prosper me in every way. As I become more of a giver, You will give me more seed to sow. Thank You Lord, that You told the farmer not to muzzle the ox. Just so, You won't have me live in deep poverty while You are abundantly blessing others through me, unless You are testing me. I love You, Lord, with all my heart. Be glorified in my life! I pray these things in the wonderful name of Jesus, Amen!!

Exodus 9:29b: . . . the earth is the LORD'S. [1]

Deuteronomy 8:18: [18]And you shall remember the LORD your God, for *it is* He who gives you power to get wealth, that He may establish His covenant which He swore to your fathers, as *it is* this day. [2]

Deuteronomy 30:8-10: [8]You will again obey the LORD and follow all his commands I am giving you today. [9]Then the LORD your God will make you most prosperous in all the work of your hands and in the fruit of your womb, the young of your livestock and the crops of your land. The LORD will again delight in you and make you prosperous, just as he delighted in your fathers, [10]if you obey the LORD your God and keep his commands and decrees that are written in this Book of the Law and turn to the LORD your God with all your heart and with all your soul. [1]

I Samuel 2:7-8: [7]The LORD sends poverty and wealth; he humbles and he exalts. [8]He raises the poor from the dust and lifts the needy from the ash heap; he seats them with princes and has them inherit a throne of honor. For the foundations of the earth are the LORD'S; upon them he has set the world. [1]

Psalms 24:1: [1]The earth is the LORD'S, and everything in it, the world, and all who live in it; [3]

Proverbs 3:9,10: [9]Honor the LORD with your wealth, with the first fruits of all your crops; [10]then your barns will be filled to overflowing, and your vats will brim over with new wine. [1]
Father, help me to honor You with everything You give me and to give freely, knowing that I have not exhausted Your supply.

Proverbs 10:22: [22]The blessing of the LORD makes *one* rich, and He adds no sorrow with it. [2]

Proverbs 13:21-22: [21]Misfortune pursues the sinner, but prosperity is the reward of the righteous. [22]A good man leaves an inheritance for his children's children, but a sinner's wealth is stored up for the righteous. [1]

Proverbs 15:6: [6]Great wealth is *in* the house of the righteous, but trouble is in the income of the wicked. [3]

Proverbs 28:25: [25]A greedy man stirs up dissension, but he who trusts in the LORD will prosper. [1]

Ecclesiastes 5:19: [19]Moreover, when God gives any man wealth and possessions, and enables him to enjoy them, to accept his lot and be happy in his work—this is a gift of God. [1]

Isaiah 45:3: [3]I will give you the treasures of darkness and hidden wealth of secret places, so that you may know that it is I, The LORD, the God of Israel, who calls you by your name. [3]

· · · · · · · · · · · ·

MARIAN'S TESTIMONY

After the unexpected death of my husband in 2006, the Lord put me in a situation that would test my faith to the very limits and would solidify in my heart the faithfulness of God forever. I was in nursing school full time, had two kids, and a mortgage of almost a thousand dollars a month. My husband had left no inheritance, insurance or benefits of any kind. The only thing I had was an income of five hundred dollars a month, a car that was on its last legs, and a whole lot of debt. I didn't know what to do except drop out of school, go back to work full-time and probably sell my house. Fortunately, God had a much better plan.

My parents divorced when I was about six years old, and I had only seen my father seven times since. To say we had an estranged relationship was an understatement. My father is not, and never has been, a Christian, but he has always been a hard worker who knows how to make and save money. During a phone conversation one afternoon, I told him the situation I was in and what I felt I had to do. He offered to pay my mortgage for sixteen months if I would continue to go to school. Now, the fact that my father had not even given me so much as a Christmas present since I was six should tell you what kind of miracle this was; close to the parting of the Red Sea!

One day after getting my car fixed, I was told by my mechanic that it was time to look for another vehicle. I went to visit my pastor's wife and she suggested I start praying for a new car, so I did. Four days later some people I had never met gave me a van. They had just bought a new van and felt God was leading them to give their old one away instead of trading it in. The day before they were to move, they were having breakfast with my pastor and his wife, and asked if they knew anyone who was in need of a used minivan! This was two weeks before Christmas and I had no money to buy my children gifts, so I was able to give my old car to my son for Christmas. (Miraculously, it has been two and a half years now and the car is still running.) The van lasted about a year. When it died, I still could not afford a new car. I prayed again. That same day someone told me they would buy me a car! They also paid for the transfer of the title, the taxes and for four new tires!!

Later, I had a couple of teeth that really needed to be capped. I had needed work done for a while, but had always put it off because I figured once I graduated and started working full time I could get them fixed. However, it didn't quite work out as I had planned. (Not much did during that time period.) I had just finished school, but had not taken my boards yet, and now my teeth were hurting and I had to get them fixed. It was going to take over fifteen hundred dollars to fix my mouth and I had just been laid off for six weeks. So I prayed. A couple of days later, I was told to go to the dentist and not to worry about the bill; it would be taken care of.

There were so many more miracles that happened during this time that it would take a whole book in itself to tell them all, so let me just say there was not a time that I was in need that God did not provide. God's Word is Truth and Life, and when He said, "Try Me," He really intends us to. I want to end with this: When I was doing my taxes for the last full year I was in nursing school, I was amazed at how much the Lord had enabled me to give in tithes and offerings! I challenge people to trust God, give whatever He tells you to give, and sit back and watch Him come through for you!

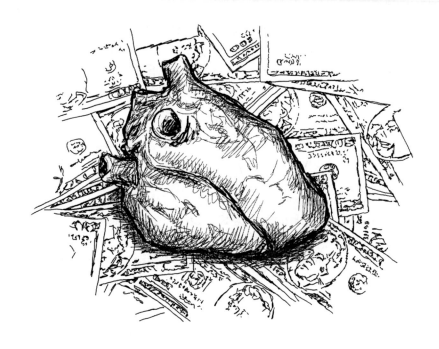

12.

WARNING — IDOLOTRY

The biggest problem regarding finances is the condition of our hearts. The love of money may translate into greed and may be expressed as a trust and hope in money to shelter and provide security. These attitudes are idolatrous. The love of money will cause insecurity or worry in one who is short of money, and pride and unteachableness in one who perceives himself as having much, or having more than others. Either the worry over insufficient funds, or the busyness (if not pride) that the purchasing and maintaining of many possessions brings, may choke out the word of God in our lives. We soon become unfruitful.

We had moved to Tennessee, and I was pastoring a new church plant. Besides four children and ourselves, we had one other family in the church. The fellowship was sweet and presence of the Lord was good. I was also a member of a pastors' fellowship that met monthly for lunch. One month, the meeting was at an especially large and successful appearing church. The pastor enjoyed showing us through the facility and told us about various programs and technology they had, and how the Lord was using them. I became more and more uncomfortable and felt painfully small in my own eyes. I didn't resent the success I was hearing about, but felt terribly unworthy to be there and call myself by the same title as the rest of the pastors. I cried out to the Lord for help and comfort. He told me that my attitude was sin and that I needed to repent. I was shocked, but did ask for forgiveness, and asked for more understanding.

When the meeting was over, I asked the Lord again for more revelation. As I cried out to Him, I felt Him saying that I was to be secure in knowing Him. If I was insecure because "my" church was small, then I would be haughty when the church was big. Either attitude reflected the same sin. I repented and confessed over and over again with relief, "Yes Lord. I do know You." Later, I found the scripture (Jer. 10:23-24) and realized that "knowing" the Lord in that verse doesn't just mean relationship, but also implies that I become like Him in character. I have since fought to work that truth into my life whenever I have felt small in my own eyes.

The same principle is true of finances. The believer who struggles with insecurity over his poverty (compared to his friends) may blame it on the simple lack of money. The feelings seem justifiable, but God wants us to be secure in Him. This man feels a victim of his poverty and believes that if he had more money, his insecurity would be solved. Just so, the believer who comes into sudden affluence may sense his own pride and blame the pride on the wealth. He would never say it out loud, but in his heart may easily say, "I'm somehow a victim of this wealth God gave me (it's really His fault). The only way out is to lose it all and I'm not willing to do that!" But it is the *love* of (the trust in and dependence on) the idol called money that is the root of the problem, not the money itself. The problem is in our own hearts and the money, or lack of it, has revealed or uncovered our heart problem. (Just as my real problem wasn't the size of my church.) The scripture is clear that our security is to be in God. We are not to make our boast in wisdom, wealth or power (or allow insecurity from the lack of these), but rather our security, trust and boast is to be in God (Jer. 9:23-24).

"Let him who boasts, boast about this: that he understands and knows me, that I am the LORD, who exercises kindness, justice and righteousness on earth, for in these I delight," declares the LORD." **Jeremiah 9:24**

My security and sense of self-esteem must come from my relationship with God, because I know Him, and because His character (His kindness, justice, and righteousness) is flowing through me. If I really know Him, then I'll trust that He will always take care of me. Only then will I overcome insecurity related to a lack of stuff or an insignificant position. Only then will I not be puffed up by the slightest blessing of money or influence. Every time I sense insecurity or pride, I say, "No, but my security is in the fact that I know Him, and that I am coming to reflect His kindness and justice and righteousness! He will always take care of me!"

For the believer, there is another appropriate course of action. Whenever we sense that money is having undue influence over us (often manifested by feelings of stinginess), we need to give. The remedy for stinginess is to give generously. We may need to give over and over, as directed or allowed by the Spirit, until we are either free from the idolatry in our heart, or out of money. Either way, the problem will be solved. Paul says it clearly.

[17]Command those who are rich in this present world not to be arrogant nor to put their hope in wealth, which is so uncertain, but to put their hope in God, who richly provides us with everything for our enjoyment. [18]Command them to do good, to be rich in good deeds, and to be generous and willing to share. [19]In this way they will lay up treasure for themselves as a firm foundation for the coming age, so that they may take hold of the life that is truly life. **I Timothy 6:17-19**[1]

Remember that almost no one feels rich, unless he has a sudden influx of money. In the normal course of affairs, the definition of rich is always someone *else* who has a lot more money than you do. The myth is that if you are rich, you can have about anything you want, anytime you want it. That is largely propaganda spread by the media and by the father of lies, the devil. The unspoken corollary is that you won't need to trust God for money anymore. Expenses and wants, however, rise (at least) proportionately with income, and taxes usually rise exponentially!

Lord, help me to have my security in You so I won't be easily puffed up by wealth, or become insecure when I have to believe You for every little need. I want to know You more. I need more of Your kindness, justice and righteousness manifested through my life. Forgive me for when I have made an idol out of money. I've sometimes put my trust in money, sometimes had more joy and longing for it than for You. I've also allowed myself to think more highly (or lowly) of myself than I ought. I reaffirm that You are my God, and no other. I purpose not to trust in anything but You. I humble myself before You and acknowledge that all good things come from You, but can disappear like a vapor. You are my safety, my health, my security and my source of provision. I trust that when all others and all else fails me that You will never leave me or forsake me. I love You. I pray these things in the name of Jesus, Amen.

Exodus 20:23: [23]You shall not make *other gods* besides Me; gods of silver or gods of gold, you shall not make for yourselves. [3]

Colossians 6:10, 11: [5]Put to death, therefore, whatever belongs to your earthly nature: sexual immorality, impurity, lust, evil desires and *greed, which is idolatry.* [6]Because of these, the wrath of God is coming. [1]

Deuteronomy 6:10-12: [10]So it shall be, when the LORD your God brings you into the land of which He swore to your fathers, to Abraham, Isaac, and Jacob, to give you large and beautiful cities which you did not build, [11]houses full of all good things, which you did not fill, hewn-out wells which you did not dig, vineyards and olive trees which you did not plant—when you have eaten and are full—[12]*then* beware, lest you forget the LORD who brought you out of the land of Egypt, from the house of bondage. [2]

Hosea 8:4b: With their silver and gold they make idols for themselves to their own destruction. [1]

Deuteronomy 31:20: [20]When I have brought them into the land flowing with milk and honey, the land I promised on oath to their forefathers, and when they eat their fill and thrive, they will turn to other gods and worship them, rejecting me and breaking my covenant. [1]
Lord, I purpose to turn away from my pride and self-sufficiency, and to seek You with all my stingy heart. I love You and desperately need You.

Job 31:24-5, 28: [24]If I have made gold my hope, or said to fine gold, "*You are* my confidence"; [25]If I have rejoiced because my wealth *was* great, and because my hand had gained much; [28]This also *would be* an iniquity *deserving of* judgment, for I would have denied God *who is* above. [2]

Psalms 52:1, 5-7: [1]Why do you boast of evil, you mighty man? Why do you boast all day long, you who are a disgrace in the eyes of God [5]Surely God will bring you down to everlasting ruin: He will snatch you up and tear you from your tent; He will uproot you from the land of the living. *Selah*
[6]The righteous will see and fear; they will laugh at Him, saying, [7]"Here now is the man who did not make God his stronghold, but trusted in his great wealth and grew strong by destroying others!" [1]

Proverbs 11:28: [28]Whoever trusts in his riches will fall, but the righteous will thrive like a green leaf. [1]

Matthew 13:22: [22]The one who received the seed that fell among the thorns is the man who hears the word, but the worries of this life and the deceitfulness of wealth choke it, making it unfruitful.[1]
Help me to see, with the help of Your Holy Spirit, how wealth and the desire for stuff have deceived me. Lord, I want to be one who bears 30 or 60 or 100 fold for Your kingdom.

Daniel 5:3-4, 23b: [3]So they brought in the gold goblets that had been taken from the temple of God in Jerusalem, and the king and his nobles, his wives and his concubines drank from them. [4]As they drank the wine, they praised the gods of gold and silver, of bronze, iron, wood and stone. [23b]You praised the gods of silver and gold, of bronze, iron, wood and stone, which cannot see or hear or understand. But you did not honor the God who holds in his hand your life and all your ways. [1]

Jeremiah 10:23-24: [23]This is what the LORD says: "Let not the wise man boast of his wisdom or the strong man boast of his strength or the rich man boast of his riches, [24]but let him who boasts, boast about this: that he understands and knows me, that I am the LORD, who exercises kindness, justice and righteousness on earth, for in these I delight," declares the LORD. [3]

Hosea 2:8, 9: [8]She has not acknowledged that I was the one who gave her the grain, the new wine and oil, who lavished on her the silver and gold— which they used for Baal. [9]Therefore I will take away my grain when it ripens, and my new wine when it is ready. I will take back my wool and my linen, intended to cover her nakedness. [1]

Hosea 4:7: [7]The more they increased *and* multiplied [in prosperity and power], the more they sinned against Me; I will change their glory into shame. [5]

Hosea 13:5-6: [5]I cared for you in the desert, in the land of burning heat. [6]When I fed them, they were satisfied; when they were satisfied, they became proud; then they forgot me. [1]

Matthew 19:22-24: [22]When the young man heard this, he went away sad, because he had great wealth.
[23]Then Jesus said to his disciples, "I tell you the truth, it is hard for a rich man to enter the kingdom of heaven. [24]Again I tell you, it is easier for a camel to go through the eye of a needle than for a rich man to enter the kingdom of God." [1]
Lord Jesus, I desperately want, not only to enter, but to also help build Your kingdom. Change my heart, Lord, and cause me to die to myself and live to You so that You can use me for Your honor and Your glory.

13.

CONDITIONS (PART I)

The blessing and prosperity of the Lord are not without conditions. He blesses those who fear and obey Him and those who put His kingdom first—those whose primary focus is not confined to the desires of the flesh and material things. Material possessions or rewards are but a byproduct of the life radically committed to the Lord. His focus regarding blessings is both for this life and for eternity. If He allows us to suffer now, it is for great eternal gain, but often (like Job) there will be a future reward here.

The conditions or requirement for each person to be blessed are according to the word of God, but are confirmed by the Spirit to each heart, as the Spirit chooses. Some conditions are quite individual.

I have the hobby of energy efficiency. We tend to have very low electric bills! In 1997, our downstairs air conditioner unit went out. It was an old inefficient model. In the process of getting estimates we discovered that the ductwork in the attic was in bad shape and needed to be reworked. (Air conditioning the attic in Georgia is a bad idea!) The quote for the least efficient model, leaving the duct-work "as is", was about half the cost of a high-efficiency (16 SEER), two-speed heat pump. The latter estimate also included complete sealing of the ductwork and zone control. I was unemployed and we had just enough money to hope for the first quote. It was summer in Georgia, and very hot and humid!

Before we could make a decision, we took our annual visit to Tulsa to visit friends and relatives there. On a Sunday after church we went with friends to eat lunch at the Olive Garden. As we perused the menu, Martha asked discreetly it if was all right if she got the Tour-of-Italy (which was the most expensive item on the menu). I was feeling quite tight financially right then (given the situation at home). I suggested that she get one of the three or four items that were on special and were about half the price of what she wanted. She graciously agreed.

A few minutes later, the Holy Spirit reminded me of a biblical financial teaching we had received about how the Lord treats husbands the way they treat their wives. Then He asked me a question I knew was loaded. "Do you want the high-efficiency, expensive heat pump quote or the economy (cheap) quote?" I kind of gasped inside. It took me a few minutes, but I finally summoned up the humility to whisper to my wife that it was all right (quite all right) if she got the Tour-of-Italy. I also apologized for my stinginess. She took me up on the offer.

I forgot about the incident and didn't tell my wife what the Lord had said, because we were with friends most of the day. On Monday morning, Martha went early as usual to have coffee with her mother.

When she got back she said she *had* to talk to me. Her mother had taken her aside and said that she just wanted to tell her that some of her four married siblings had come into financial difficulty. She and Martha's dad (Poppo) had helped each of them in turn with the same amount of money. They had a policy that if they helped any of their six children, they would help each of the others with the same amount, sort of as part of their inheritance. She *knew* we didn't need any money, but just felt that she should tell us while we were there just in case we developed a need in the future! The amount that was available to us was the difference between the high-efficiency system and the "economy" one. Praise the Lord! I was never so glad that the Lord had spoken to my heart and that I had obeyed. God is so good.

Lord, show me the ways in which I fail to please You, where I fail to meet the conditions for Your full blessing on my life. I want to bring pleasure to Your heart, and glory to Your name. I know You love to bless and provide for me. You are my Father, and You see the end from the beginning. Help me to focus on what is of eternal value, and yet expect You, my precious Lord, to bless me and to provide for my needs. Thank you for all the wonderful blessings You've already given me! In Your name I pray, Amen.

Deuteronomy 4:1: [1]Hear now, O Israel, the decrees and laws I am about to teach you. Follow them so that you may live and may go in and take possession of the land that the Lord, the God of your fathers, is giving you. [1]

Deuteronomy 4:40: [40]Keep his decrees and commands, which I am giving you today, so that it may go well with you and your children after you and that you may live long in the land the LORD your God gives you for all time. [1]

Deuteronomy 15:4: [4]However, there should be no poor among you, for in the land the LORD your God is giving you to possess as your inheritance, he will richly bless you, [5]if only you fully obey the LORD your God and are careful to follow all these commands I am giving you today. [6]For the LORD your God will bless you as he has promised, and you will lend to many nations, but will borrow from none. You will rule over many nations, but none will rule over you. [1]

Deuteronomy 29:9: [9]So keep the words of this covenant to do them, that you may prosper in all that you do. [3]

Joshua 1:7-9: [7]Only be strong and very courageous, that you may observe to do according to all the law which Moses My servant commanded you; do not turn from it to the right hand or to the left, that you may prosper wherever you go. [8]This Book of the Law shall not depart from your mouth, but you shall meditate in it day and night, that you may observe to do according to all that is written in it. For then you will make your way prosperous, and then you will have good success. [9]Have I not commanded you? Be strong and of good courage; do not be afraid, nor be dismayed, for the LORD your God *is* with you wherever you go. [2]

Job 2:3: [3]The LORD said to Satan, "Have you considered My servant Job? For there is no one like him on the earth, a blameless and upright man fearing God and turning away from evil. And he still holds fast his integrity, although you incited Me against him to ruin him without cause." [3]

Job 41:10, 12-13: [10]And the LORD restored Job's losses [made him prosperous again[1]] when he prayed for his friends. Indeed the LORD gave Job twice as much as he had before.[2] [12]The LORD blessed the latter *days* of Job more than his beginning; and he had 14,000 sheep and 6,000 camels and 1,000 yoke of oxen and 1,000 female donkeys. [13]He had seven sons and three daughters.[3]

Deuteronomy 6:17: [17]You should diligently keep the commandments of the LORD your God, and His testimonies and His statutes which He has commanded you. [18]You shall do what is right and good in the sight of the LORD, that it may be well with you and that you may go in and possess the good land which the LORD swore to *give* your fathers, [19]by driving out all your enemies from before you, as the LORD has spoken. [3]

Psalms 101:6: [6]My eyes shall be upon the faithful of the land, that they may dwell with me; He who walks in a blameless way is the one who will minister to me. [1]

Psalms 127:1,2: [1] Except the LORD builds the house, they labor in vain who build it; Except the LORD keeps the city, the watchman wakes but in vain. [2]It is vain for you to rise up early, to take rest late, to eat the bread of [anxious] toil; For He gives [blessings] to His beloved in sleep.[5]

Psalms 128:1-4: [1]Blessed are all who fear the LORD, who walk in his ways. [2]You will eat the fruit of your labor; blessings and prosperity will be yours. [3]Your wife will be like a fruitful vine within your house; your sons will be like olive shoots around your table. [4]Thus is the man blessed who fears the LORD. [1]

· · · · · · · · · · ·

Testimony of Terry

Two years ago I was working with my brother for his father-in-law who lives on the coast. I had just gotten home and walked into my closet to change my clothes. I had been gone for a week or so. We were in financial need, and I felt impressed to make a "withdrawal" from my heavenly bank account while standing in the closet. I told the Lord, "I'm withdrawing $10,000 from that account." I noted in my prayer journal that it was March 15th. Across the years virtually all of our investments have been heavenward. Jesus told us to store up treasure in heaven, so that's what Debbie and I have done. I don't ever remember making this type of withdrawal before, but I knew in my heart I could receive this amount by faith.

On May 4 (less than two months later), we unexpectedly received a check of $12,000 from an individual we had known for many years. We had never received this large an amount of money before. Needless to say, we gave much thanks to the Lord!

Several years back (before this incident), we knew we were going to be in transition from one area of ministry to another in the near future, but had no idea what it would be. Debbie and I gave a very large amount of money to another ministry as a seed toward our future need. We have experienced the fruit of that seed to this very day. The principal of sowing and reaping is ever so true. The scripture tells us, "Give and it will be given to you good measure pressed down, shaken together and running over shall *men pour into your lap (Luke 6:38)*." The money is in the earth and the Lord uses people to bring it to us.

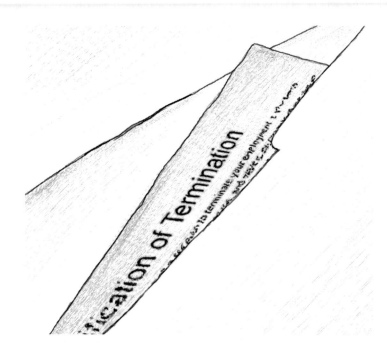

14.

PROMISES

The Lord has given us many wonderful promises in scripture. Some promises are for everyone ("delight yourself in the Lord and He will give you the desires of your heart," Psalms 37:4). Other scriptural promises are quickened to us by the Spirit at a particular time. Still other promises may not be exact wording of scripture, but the Spirit whispers them in our hearts and we know they are for us. For all the promises that we receive, however, after getting confirmation (if it is a major promise), we must hold on to the promise in faith. Sometimes we know a promise is meant for us, but not at the time it is given (not yet), and we believe by faith for its realization in the future. In some cases we must pray to receive the promises. In other cases we must also sow towards receiving the promise. At other times, however, we just believe. If we ask, the Lord will give us wisdom to know which is which.

Promises are important for us to cling to when times are hard, just as Abraham clung to the promise that God would provide a son. It is by faith that we please God. Jesus told His disciples that he would suffer, die and on the third day rise again. When the angel spoke to the two Marys, he said, "He has risen, just *as He said.*" We can trust that if Jesus *rose up from the dead* according to what He told us, then in every other promise He has given us, He will do **JUST AS HE SAID!**

During the earlier years of my time in Georgia, I had a boss who became mentally unstable. One Saturday, I was called into the office and given my severance papers (the pink slip)! My wife and I were in shock and didn't know what to do or where to turn. My pastor and another man of God came over with their wives to minister to us. During the course of the evening, each of the men said separately that they believed they were hearing from the Lord that one day I would own the practice. It seemed preposterous to me, since I had just been fired, but I believed God as much as I could.

Early Sunday morning my boss called me and told me to report to work Monday morning. He told me that he had just wanted to let me know who the boss was. I got to practice forgiveness. I never forgot the promise, but never prayed for it, because to pray for it was to pray against my boss. I knew I had to be loyal to him like David was loyal to King Saul, and I couldn't pray against him. Two years later, through a series of incredible miracles, I did "inherit" the practice. The fact that I had been fired actually worked to my great advantage, since my contract had never been reinstated. I became "the boss" and the man who had fired me worked for me. God is an awesome God.

Lord, I thank you for Your promises. I thank you that You want to prosper and bless me, as much as I can handle. I believe You will provide for me, and give me sufficient finances so I can bless others at every opportunity. I believe You will protect me. I will not be afraid of the terror by night, nor of the arrow that flies by day, nor of the pestilence that walks in darkness, nor of the destruction that lays waste at noonday. A thousand may fall at my side, and ten thousand at my right hand; but it shall not come near me. I am the head and not the tail. I am blessed going in and going out. As I delight myself in You, You will give me the desires of my heart. You desire to bless and prosper me in every area of my life, as I yield myself to You, and search after You. I choose to seek You first. I desire to be blessed so that I can be the blessing to others that You have called me to be. Show me which of Your promises I am to claim now, and which ones are for the future. In Jesus' name I pray, Amen!

Leviticus 26:3-5, 6, 9-11: [3]If you walk in My statutes and keep My commandments so as to carry them out, [4]then I shall give you rains in their season, so that the land will yield its produce and the trees of the field will bear their fruit. [5]Indeed, your threshing will last for you until grape gathering, and grape gathering will last until sowing time. You will thus eat your food to the full and live securely in your land. [6]I shall also grant peace in the land, so that you may lie down with no one making *you* tremble. I shall also eliminate harmful beasts from the land, and no sword will pass through your land . . . [9]So I will turn toward you and make you fruitful and multiply you, and I will confirm My covenant with you. [10]You will eat the old supply and clear out the old because of the new. [11]Moreover, I will make My dwelling among you, and My soul will not reject you. [12]I will also walk among you and be your God, and you shall be My people.[3]

Deuteronomy 8:6-10: [6]Therefore, you shall keep the commandments of the LORD your God, to walk in His ways and to fear Him. [7]For the LORD your God is bringing you into a good land, a land of brooks of water, of fountains and springs, flowing forth in valleys and hills; [8]a land of wheat and barley, of vines and fig trees and pomegranates, a land of olive oil and honey; [9]a land where you will eat food without scarcity, in which you will not lack anything; a land whose stones are iron, and out of whose hills you can dig copper. [10]When you have eaten and are satisfied, you shall bless the LORD your God for the good land which He has given you. [1]

Deuteronomy 15:6: [6]For the LORD your God will bless you as he has promised, and you will lend to many nations, but will borrow from none. You will rule over many nations, but none will rule over you.[1]

Deuteronomy 30:9-10: [9]Then the LORD your God will make you most prosperous in all the work of your hands and in the fruit of your womb, the young of your livestock and the crops of your land. The LORD will again delight in you and make you prosperous, just as he delighted in your fathers, [10]if you obey the LORD your God and keep his commands and decrees that are written in this Book of the Law and turn to the LORD your God with all your heart and with all your soul. [1]

I Samuel 2:7: [7]The LORD makes poor and rich; He brings low, He also exalts. [3]

Job 23:10: [10]But He knows the way I take; *when* He has tried me, I shall come forth as gold. [3]

Psalms 34:8-10, 19: [8]Oh, taste and see that the LORD *is* good; Blessed *is* the man *who* trusts in Him! [9]Oh, fear the LORD, you His saints! *There is* no want to those who fear Him. [10]The young lions lack and suffer hunger; but those who seek the LORD shall not lack any good *thing . . .* [19]Many are the afflictions of the righteous, but the LORD delivers him out of them all. [3]

Psalms 37:4-7, 11: [4]Delight yourself in the LORD; and He will give you the desires of your heart. [5]Commit your way to the LORD, trust also in Him, and He will do it. [6]He will bring forth your righteousness as the light and your judgment as the noonday. [7]Rest in the LORD and wait patiently for Him; do not fret because of him who prospers in his way, because of the man who carries out wicked schemes . . . [11]But the humble will inherit the land and will delight themselves in abundant prosperity. [3]

Psalms 50:14-15: [14]Offer to God a sacrifice of thanksgiving and pay your vows to the Most High; [15]Call upon Me in the day of trouble; I shall rescue you, and you will honor Me. [3]

Psalms 113:7-9: [7]He raises the poor from the dust and lifts the needy from the ash heap, [8]To make *them* sit with princes, with the princes of His people. [9]He makes the barren woman abide in the house *as* a joyful mother of children. Praise the LORD! [3]

Psalms 115:14-15: [14]May the LORD give you increase, you and your children. [15]May you be blessed of the LORD, Maker of heaven and earth. [3]

Psalms 122:7: [7]May peace be within your walls, and prosperity within your palaces. [3]

Proverbs 2:6: [6]For the LORD gives wisdom; From His mouth *come* knowledge and understanding. [7]He stores up sound wisdom for the upright; *He is* a shield to those who walk in integrity, [8]Guarding the paths of justice, and He preserves the way of His godly ones. [2]

Proverbs 10:22: [22]The blessing of the LORD, it makes [truly] rich, and He adds no sorrow with it, *neither* does toiling increase it. [5]

Proverbs 13:22: [22]A good *man* leaves an inheritance to his children's children, but the wealth of the sinner is stored up for the righteous. [3]

Proverbs 21:20: [20]There is precious treasure and oil in the dwelling of the wise, but a foolish man swallows it up. [1]

Proverbs 28:8: [8]He who increases his wealth by interest and usury gathers it for him who is gracious to the poor. [1]

Proverbs 28:20: [20]A faithful man will abound with blessings, but he who makes haste to be rich will not go unpunished. [3]

Proverbs 28:25: [25]An arrogant man stirs up strife, but he who trusts in the LORD will prosper. [3]

· · · · · · · · · ·

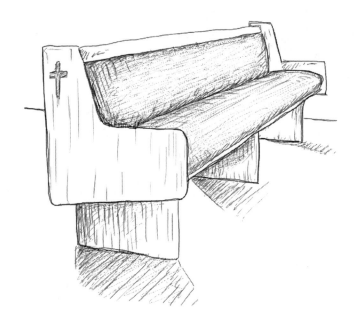

PASTOR DAN'S TESTIMONY

I pastor a small church in east Tennessee. Several years ago we were looking at a building right on the main street of our small town. The owner was asking $59,000 for it, but the Lord told me to offer $29,000. The realtor laughed at me and said there was no way we could get it for anywhere close to that. I told him to put in our offer anyway. He came back and said the owner laughed, too, and said she had decided to take it off the market and use it for something else if it didn't sell by the end of the week for something close to her asking price. I met with two brothers from the church to pray, and the Lord again told each of us that we were to offer $29,000. The realtor reluctantly took the offer back to the owner, who again turned it down flat. Three days later he called me back.

"You won't believe this," he said.

"Oh, yes, I will," I replied. "What is it?"

"The owner says she's afraid NOT to give it to you for $29,000!"

Praise the Lord! He is so faithful! But that's not the end of the story. We put in a great deal of time and sweat to make the building useable. When we were able to start meeting there, we had no furnishings but a few old rickety folding chairs. We decided that it would be nice to at least have some pews. We started praying.

A pastor friend of mine in Florida invited me to come preach at his church. Knowing he had lots of connections, I asked him if he knew anyone who had pews for sale. He told me that in his twenty years in the area, he had never heard of one person having pews available.

When I got down there, my pastor friend told me, "You're not going to believe this…"

I said, "Yes, I will. What's up?"

Well, a pastor had called him after trying unsuccessfully to contact several other churches. He had pews he needed to get rid of! I told my wife, Sharon, that we would know this was our answer to prayer if the pews turned out to be eleven feet long, which was the size we needed for our sanctuary. She told me she didn't think they made pews that size – they were usually ten or twelve feet.

We went to see the pews and they were eleven feet, three inches long! (This turned out to be the perfect size for our building.) There were exactly as many as we needed, too. The pastor said he wouldn't take any money for them; he just wanted them to go to the Lord's work. Then he said, "What about this other stuff?" It turns out that two churches had merged, and they had all the furnishings for a whole church that they wanted to give us!

They gave us a pulpit, an overhead projector with worship overheads, tables, collection and communion plates, nursery and Sunday School materials and supplies – even carved wooden signs for the bathroom doors! – everything we needed! Then the pastor said, "Do you need an amp for a bass guitar?"

I said, "Sure. We don't have a bass guitar, but I can believe God for one."   The next time I saw my other pastor friend, I shared this story with him. He laughed, went into another room, came back and handed me a bass guitar. He told me they had just gotten a new one. "Apparently God meant this one for you," he said.

I had to rent a U-Haul to bring all the blessings home. At the last meeting I preached down there, my pastor friend shared our testimony of God's great blessing on us with the congregation, and suggested that maybe they could help with the U-Haul rental. As people were leaving, they pressed money into my hands and pockets. When we counted it out after the service, we were only twelve dollars short of the rental fee. The pastor reached in his pocket and took out a twenty dollar bill. He declared, "Never let it be said that what God supplies is not enough." To which I say, AMEN and AMEN!

By the way, that's not the end of the story, either. We used the pews for eight years until they started to fall apart, and then we prayed for some chairs. Just recently the Lord provided a whole church full of padded, interlocking chairs—exactly what we were praying for, at no charge. He also provided a beautiful, plexi-glass pulpit to replace the homemade one. His faithfulness never ends!

15.

CONTENTMENT

The Lord requires thankfulness and contentment with what He has given me. This does not mean I throw away my dreams and the desires of my heart. I am to be grateful for what He has provided, and see the value in it (in the natural and in what it does for my character). At the same time, I am to keep my faith alive, that at the right time He will fulfill the desires and visions He has placed in my heart. As I yield my longings to Him and place them on the altar, He is freed to give me the things He desires for me. He'll give them to me in His time and in His way. As a result, there will be no sorrow *from*, and no bondage *to* the possessions, jobs, ministries and people He places in my life.

As a single medical student, I had $500 per month to cover every-thing but tuition and books (tithes and offerings, rent, utilities, food, gas, etc.). By being very frugal I was able to make it, but there was little extra.

From time to time we were invited to professors' houses for meals or just get-togethers, which were a great blessing. On one of those occasions, one of my classmates asked a question that was also on my heart. He was troubled because we were always on the receiving end of such generosity. While we appreciated it greatly, we struggled with some guilt from time to time, feeling like we had nothing to give in return. The professor laughed lightheartedly and told us not to worry. He had felt the same way when he was in our shoes. He let us know that life has seasons. "Your season to give will come," he said. "You won't be giving back to us, but will be giving to oth-ers. Just like you, many of the people you bless won't be able to pay you back and it won't bother you at all. You will be passing on the blessing, and they in turn will pass it on to others."

His glad-hearted response brought peace to me. It also brought a determination to have the same giving heart whenever the Lord allowed it. Sometimes in life we can bless those who have blessed us, and that is good and proper. Many times, however, we have no way to repay those who sow into our lives. Instead, we later pass along the blessing to others, who in turn have no way to repay us. It is the way of the Kingdom of God.

Lord, thank you for my situation and for what You have given me. Thank you for the people You have put in my life. Use my circum-stances to work Your character in me and work gratefulness in my heart. Help me to embrace each season that you bring into my life. I want to receive graciously when You cause others to bless me, but even more, I want to be a blessing to others, as You permit, expect-ing nothing in return from them. I trust that in due time, You will grant me the desires of my heart that come from You. I desire that when you grant them, You will bring glory to Your name and advance to Your kingdom as a result. Protect me from idolatry. I pray these things in Jesus' name, Amen.

Job 1:21, 22: ²¹And he said: "Naked I came from my mother's womb, and naked shall I return there. The LORD gave, and the LORD has taken away; blessed be the name of the LORD." ²²In all this Job did not sin nor charge God with wrong. ¹

Job 2:10: ¹⁰He replied, "You are talking like a foolish woman. Shall we accept good from God, and not trouble?" In all this, Job did not sin in what he said. ¹ *(The Hebrew word rendered foolish implies moral deficiency.)*

Psalms 37:16, 17: ¹⁶Better the little that the righteous have than the wealth of many wicked; ¹⁷for the power of the wicked will be broken, but the LORD upholds the righteous. ¹

Psalms 73:25-26, 28: ²⁵Whom have I in Heaven but You? And I have no delight *or* desire on earth besides You. ²⁶ My flesh and my heart may fail, but God is the Rock *and* firm strength of my heart, and my portion forever. ⁵ ²⁸But *it is* good for me to draw near to God; I have put my trust in the Lord GOD, that I may declare all Your works. ²

Psalms 119:57: ⁵⁷You are my portion, O LORD; I have promised to obey your words. ¹

Proverbs 13:7-8: ⁷One man pretends to be rich, yet has nothing; another pretends to be poor, yet has great wealth. ⁸A man's riches may ransom his life, but a poor man hears no threat. ¹

Proverbs 15:16: ⁶Better a little with the fear of the LORD than great wealth with turmoil. ¹
Holy Spirit, please show me when things I want will only bring trouble, business and turmoil to my life.

Proverbs 30:7-9: ⁷Two *things* I request of You (deprive me not before I die): ⁸Remove falsehood and lies far from me; Give me neither poverty nor riches— Feed me with the food allotted to me; ⁹Lest I be full and deny *You,* and say, "Who *is* the LORD?" Or lest I be poor and steal, and profane the name of my God. ²

Ecclesiastes 5:10-12: [10]Whoever loves money never has money enough; whoever loves wealth is never satisfied with his income. This too is meaningless. [11]As goods increase, so do those who consume them. And what benefit are they to the owner except to feast his eyes on them? [12]The sleep of a laborer is sweet, whether he eats little or much, but the abundance of a rich man permits him no sleep. 1/3

Isaiah 55:1-2: [1]Ho! Everyone who thirsts, come to the waters; and you who have no money come, buy and eat. Come, buy wine and milk without money and without cost. [2]Why do you spend money for what is not bread, and your wages for what does not satisfy? Listen carefully to Me, and eat what is good, and delight yourself in abundance. 3

Matthew 6:24-26: [24]No one can serve two masters; for either he will hate the one and love the other, or else he will be loyal to the one and despise the other. You cannot serve God and mammon.
[25]Therefore I say to you, do not worry about your life, what you will eat or what you will drink; nor about your body, what you will put on. Is not life more than food and the body more than clothing? [26]Look at the birds of the air, for they neither sow nor reap nor gather into barns; yet your heavenly Father feeds them. Are you not of more value than they? [27]Which of you by worrying can add one cubit to his stature? 2

Acts 20:33-35: [33]I have not coveted anyone's silver or gold or clothing. [34]You yourselves know that these hands of mine have supplied my own needs and the needs of my companions. [35]In everything I did, I showed you that by this kind of hard work we must help the weak, remembering the words the Lord Jesus himself said: 'It is more blessed to give than to receive.' 3

II Corinthians 6:10: [10]...sorrowful, yet always rejoicing; poor, yet making many rich; having nothing, and yet possessing everything. 1

Philippians 4:11-13: [11]Not that I speak from want, for I have learned to be content in whatever circumstances I am. [12]I know how to get along with humble means, and I also know how to live in prosperity;

in any and every circumstance I have learned the secret of being filled and going hungry, both of having abundance and suffering need. [13]I can do all things through Him who strengthens me. [3]

Colossians 3:2: [2]Set your mind on the things above, not on the things that are on earth. [3]

I Thessalonians 5:16-18: [16]Be joyful always; [17]pray continually; [18]give thanks in all circumstances, for this is God's will for you in Christ Jesus.[1]

I Timothy 3:3: [3]...not addicted to wine or pugnacious, but gentle, peaceable, free from the love of money. [3]

I Timothy 6:6-11: [6]But godliness *actually* is a means of great gain when accompanied by contentment. [7]For we have brought nothing into the world, so we cannot take anything out of it either. [8]If we have food and covering, with these we shall be content. [9]But those who want to get rich fall into temptation and a snare, and many foolish and harmful desires which plunge men into ruin and destruction. [10]For the love of money is a root of all sorts of evil, and some by longing for it have wandered away from the faith and pierced themselves with many griefs. [11]But flee from these things, you man of God, and pursue righteousness, godliness, faith, love, perseverance *and* gentleness. [3]

Hebrews 13:5, 6: [5]*Make sure that* your character is free from the love of money, being content with what you have; for He Himself has said, "I WILL NEVER DESERT YOU, NOR WILL I EVER FORSAKE YOU," [6]so that we confidently say, "THE LORD IS MY HELPER, I WILL NOT BE AFRAID. WHAT WILL MAN DO TO ME?" [3]

I Peter 3:3-4: [3]Your beauty should not come from outward adornment, such as braided hair and the wearing of gold jewelry and fine clothes. [4]Instead, it should be that of your inner self, the unfading beauty of a gentle and quiet spirit, which is of great worth in God's sight. [1]

I John 2:16-17: [16]For all that is in the world, the lust of the flesh and the lust of the eyes and the boastful pride of life, is not from the Father, but is from the world. [17]The world is passing away, and *also* its lusts; but the one who does the will of God lives forever. [1]

16.

BLESSINGS

The Bible reveals many wonderful promises of blessing, some of which relate to prosperity and financial plenty. Often God's promises come with conditions that we must first fulfill. We must be attuned to the leadership of the Holy Spirit to claim the particular blessings the Lord has for us.

While in college in Tampa, Florida, I attended a men's retreat in Daytona Beach. The worship was wonderful and 600 men lifted their voices to the Lord. I was especially blessed by the music of a young man who played the violin with the worship team. He seemed to soar with the moving of the Spirit. I felt a great desire rise up in me to learn to play the violin, and asked the Lord to bring it to pass. When I prayed, I felt that it was His will. I had no violin or money, and didn't begin to know where to get lessons.

Nearly a year later, I came in contact with a music major who took piano through the university. I remembered the desire God had placed in my heart to learn to play the violin, and asked if they offered violin lessons. She said yes, and that they might even supply the violin! Within a few days, before I was able to follow up with the university, I discovered that a church member was moving to California. He had majored in conducting and had nearly every kind of orchestral instrument. He had two violins that he was selling for half what he paid for them. The one I chose had been broken. It had been a $120 violin that he got for $60 and then repaired. He was asking $29 for it, which I gladly paid. I then purchased a case which cost more than the violin!

I contacted the university and was soon able to start violin lessons. The first quarter I took group lessons and then the professor allowed me to continue with private lessons with him. This cost me all of $15 per quarter for a one-hour weekly lesson with one of the university's best violinists (who did national concert tours every year). One of the sisters in the church told me early on that she was praying that God would allow me to progress so quickly that I would know it was Him and not my talent.

After one quarter of private lessons, I visited my parents in Africa and brought my violin to practice. While fooling around, I discovered that if I held my double-jointed left thumb a certain (wrong) way I could make vibrato and improve the sound dramatically. When I returned to Tampa, I began playing in our small church, to everyone's delight (including mine).

The upshot of the story is that the Lord planted a desire and then a promise in my heart. Then at the right time, He provided a wonderful violin for almost nothing, and provided lessons from one of the best instructors in the area, for almost nothing. Finally, He provided me with an abnormal double-jointed left (not right) thumb. As a result, I could make the instrument play beautifully in less than nine months with techniques that I would not have normally learned for three years! God is good, and yes, it was all Him!

Lord, I thank you that I am blessed by You. You desire me to believe that You want to bless me greatly, while the enemy wants me to expect you to be harsh and mean. He knows that my negative expectations of You may be self-fulfilling, while my faith in Your great love and desire to bless me releases You to do just that. Please prompt me by Your Spirit to know which of these promises of blessing You want for my life now and give me faith to reach out and believe You for them. Convict me, I pray, to see what things or attitudes in my life are wrong and are preventing You from blessing me the way You want to. Thank you for Your great and wonderful love for me. I pray in Jesus' name, Amen.

Genesis 26:3: (The Lord to Isaac . . .) [3]"Dwell in this land, and I will be with you and bless you; for to you and your descendants I give all these lands, and I will perform the oath which I swore to Abraham your father." [2]
Lord, show me my land, my territory spiritually and naturally, and help me to be faithful there.

Genesis 26:12-14: [12]Now Isaac sowed in that land and reaped in the same year a hundredfold. And the LORD blessed him, [13]and the man became rich, and continued to grow richer until he became very wealthy; [14]for he had possessions of flocks and herds and a great household, so that the Philistines envied him. [3]

Genesis 33:10a, 11: (Jacob on meeting Esau) [10]But Jacob replied, "No, I beg of you, if now I have found favor in your sight, receive my gift that I am presenting . . . [11]"Accept, I beg of you, my blessing *and* gift that I have brought to you; for God has dealt graciously with me and I have everything." And he kept urging him and he accepted it. [5]

Genesis 39:2-6: [2]The LORD was with Joseph and he prospered, and he lived in the house of his Egyptian master. [3]When his master saw that *the LORD was with him and that the LORD gave him success in everything he did*, [4]Joseph found favor in his eyes and became his attendant. Potiphar put him in charge of his household, and he entrusted to his care everything he owned. [5]*From the time he put him in charge of his household and of all that he owned, the LORD blessed the household of the Egyptian because of Joseph. The blessing of the LORD was on everything Potiphar had, both in the house and in the field.* [6]So he left in Joseph's care everything he had; with Joseph in charge, he did not concern himself with anything except the food he ate.[1]

Deuteronomy 28:12, 13: (Moses to the Israelites) [12]The LORD will open the heavens, the storehouse of his bounty, to send rain on your land in season and to bless all the work of your hands. You will lend to many nations, but will borrow from none. [13]The LORD will make you the head, not the tail. If you pay attention to the commands of the LORD your God that I give you this day and carefully follow them, you will always be at the top, never at the bottom. [1]

Deuteronomy 29:9: [9]So keep the words of this covenant to do them, that you may prosper in all that you do. [3]

Deuteronomy 30:8-11: [8]You will again obey the LORD and follow all his commands I am giving you today. [9]Then the LORD your God will make you most prosperous in all the work of your hands and in the fruit of your womb, the young of your livestock and the crops of your land. *The LORD will again delight in you and make you prosperous*, just as he delighted in your fathers, [10]if you obey the LORD your God and keep his commands and decrees that are written in this Book of the Law and turn to the LORD your God with all your heart and with all your soul. [11]Now what I am commanding you today is not too difficult for you or beyond your reach.[1]

Joshua 1:6-9: (The Lord to Joshua) "[6]Be strong and of good courage, for to this people you shall divide as an inheritance the land which I swore to their fathers to give them. [7]Only be strong and very courageous, that you may observe to do according to all the law which Moses My servant commanded you; do not turn from it to the right hand or to the left, that you may prosper wherever you go. *8This Book of the Law shall not depart from your mouth, but you shall meditate in it day and night, that you may observe to do according to all that is written in it. For then you will make your way prosperous, and then you will have good success.* 9Have I not commanded you? Be strong and of good courage; do not be afraid, nor be dismayed, for the LORD your God *is* with you wherever you go." 2

Ruth 2:12: (Boaz to Ruth) "12The LORD repay your work, and a full reward be given you by the LORD God of Israel, under whose wings you have come for refuge." 2

Ruth 4:11: 11All the people who were in the court, and the elders, said *(to Boaz)*, "*We are* witnesses. May the LORD make the woman who is coming into your home like Rachel and Leah, both of whom built the house of Israel; and may you achieve wealth in Ephrathah and become famous in Bethlehem." 3

I Samuel 2:30b: 30*Those who honor me I will honor*, but those who despise me will be disdained. 1

Psalms 1:1-3: 1How blessed is the man who does not walk in the counsel of the wicked, nor stand in the path of sinners, nor sit in the seat of scoffers! 2But his delight is in the law of the LORD, and in His law he meditates day and night. 3He will be like a tree *firmly* planted by streams of water, which yields its fruit in its season and its leaf does not wither; and in whatever he does, he prospers. 3
Lord, convict me of when I have listened to and heeded the world's way of thinking and living, and where I have become skeptical. Help me to delight in and meditate on Your word instead, so my mind is renewed and my spirit strengthened, and so You can bless me.

Psalms 37:28-29: 28For the LORD loves the just and will not forsake his faithful ones. They will be protected forever, but the offspring of the wicked will be cut off; 29the righteous will inherit the land and dwell in it forever. 1

Psalms 127:3-5: [3]Behold, children are a gift of the LORD; the fruit of the womb is a reward. [4]Like arrows in the hand of a warrior, so are the children of one's youth. [5]How blessed is the man whose quiver is full of them; they will not be ashamed when they speak with their enemies in the gate. [3]

Proverbs 28:20: [20]A faithful man will abound with blessings, but he who hastens to be rich will not go unpunished. [2]

Holy Spirit, expose areas where I'm less than fully faithful to You, to the work You have for me, and to Your church. Deliver me from a get rich quick, greedy spirit, I pray.

Proverbs 31:10: [10]A wife of noble character who can find? She is worth far more than rubies. [1]

Proverbs 18:22: [18]He who finds a wife finds what is good and receives favor from the LORD. [1]

Proverbs 19:14: [14]Houses and wealth are inherited from parents, but a prudent wife is from the LORD.[1]

Jeremiah 17:7, 8: [7]Blessed *is* the man who trusts in the LORD, and whose hope is the LORD. [8]For he shall be like a tree planted by the waters, which spreads out its roots by the river, and will not fear when heat comes; but its leaf will be green, and will not be anxious in the year of drought, nor will cease from yielding fruit. [2]

Lord, please expose for me areas where I've put trust and hope in others, which rightfully belongs only in You. You alone are my source, my joy, my hope, and my fulfillment.

· · · · · · · · · ·

Testimony of Roger and Judith

For all the promises of God in him *are* yea, and in him Amen. [2 Corinthians 1:20 4]

My wife Judith and I were living in a small town while ministering in a neighboring city. (Two years earlier I had taken early retirement to enter into the ministry.) The commute was about twelve miles one way, and I was making the round trip twice and sometimes three times a day. We began to pray about moving.

On a cool February day in 2000 we decided to drive through a neighborhood with many condos and townhouses. Our heart's desire had been to live in a condo and we had been looking off and on for several years, but were unable to find anything affordable. We found nothing of interest and took an unfamiliar street out of the neighborhood. That's when we saw it!

We never knew these condo units existed, but as we rounded a curve and saw them we had to investigate. The first building's units were all occupied, but the second building still had four unfinished condos.

A woman "happened" to be outside. Carol lived in the one finished unit of the second building and she was a realtor. She let us into the unit beside hers and we fell in love with the place.

We began to pray and God began to answer. At first it was only an assurance within us, and then He began to give us scripture after scripture, speaking to us through His Word, telling us this place would be our home. Our excitement grew each day.

We stepped out in faith by approaching our new-found realtor and friend, asking her to put our present home on the market and to contact the owner of the condo with our offer. He turned us down.

We received word that another person was making an offer on "our" condo. We panicked. Knowing that God wanted us to have this place, we decided that He needed our help to do it (the Abraham, Hagar and Ishmael trick). In the panic of thinking someone was about to buy "our" condo, we called our realtor instructing her to offer the owner his asking price. He turned us down again!

Soon afterwards I left to join some friends on a ten-day mission trip to Haiti. My wife stayed home by herself to tend to our "condo problem." The day after my return our realtor showed up on our doorstep. She said, "I have great news! The builder went bankrupt and the unfinished condos will be auctioned off!" This did not sound like "great news" to us. It sounded devastating.

The auction date was set, a tent was erected on the property and our nerves were as taut as an overstretched bow. There were numerous people there to bid on the four units and a parcel of land.

The bidding began with each piece to be sold as a single parcel and "our" unit went first. Boy, were we ever praying! There was an opening bid by someone and our realtor immediately countered with a bid. The gavel dropped and the unit was ours ... almost! The other units had to sell as well, but even with our offer accepted we were still sweating bullets.

God came through and we went out rejoicing. He gave us the desire of our hearts.

As we walked away from the auction, I struck up a conversation with a gentleman who told me that he had come to the auction with the intent to buy "our" unit. He seemed somewhat puzzled as he said, "I came to buy that unit and for some reason I didn't even bid on it." Why he didn't bid may have puzzled him, but it didn't puzzle my wife and me.

We actually bought the condo for forty-four thousand dollars less than what we offered the owner for it. God is good! But the story isn't over.

We had a contract on the condo, but we had not yet sold our home. We began to pray more earnestly about this, because we could not pay for our new condo without first selling the house! The following day as I read the story of Joshua leading the Israelites across the Jordan River, I came to the scripture where God told Joshua to prepare, *for in three days they would pass over the river to possess their new land* (Joshua 1:11). My heart leaped! I knew God was speaking to me and I claimed it by faith. On the third day we received an offer and sold the house.

Jehovah-Jireh is but one of God's many names. Like all the rest, it is a name we can count on!

17.

HUMILITY

We had about a month after my graduation from medical school before we moved to Tampa for me to begin my residency in pathology. Without more training, my new M.D. wasn't worth much as far as making money. My new wife, Martha, was doing temporary secretarial work, and some church friends of ours invited me to work for/with them in their house cleaning business. We needed the money, and I thought it would be good for me, so I said yes. I spent a few days that week helping them clean some rather large homes. Often I was assigned to vacuuming, and cleaning the bathrooms (less skilled labor required!).

On the Friday night of my first week on the job, the graduating medical school class was invited with their spouses to a congratulations and farewell celebration. The party was held at the home of the Dean of the Medical School, an unheard of honor. I hurried home from work and showered and dressed for the occasion. Imagine my surprise when Martha and I arrived and I recognized that the large home was the one that I had cleaned just a few hours before. I was hoping I had done a good job! I was also hoping not to be embarrassed by the hostess, who was gracious, even though she recognized me and laughed. I felt somehow that I had passed a test in the spirit, and was glad I had not imagined myself too good for the work.

Humility is absolutely essential for going on in God. It is required for receiving nearly everything He has for us, yet we live in a society in which pride is the norm. In the world, and even in many churches, moderate humility, and even false humility are celebrated as though they were great humility. Yet, neither the world nor the church should be our standard, but Jesus Christ.

We do not receive humility passively, by prayer, but rather by asking the Lord to help *us* humble *ourselves*. True humility is evidenced by obedience. When you seek for true humility, look for acts of obedience which require you to actively humble yourself. For dads, washing dishes or changing dirty diapers may be active works of developing humility. Confessing faults and weaknesses in an appropriate safe place is another act that helps to humble our souls. Since pride cuts off God's grace, and humility restores it, humility is worth searching for diligently. Try to develop physical habits and thought patterns that will remind you of truth. Pride is always based on lies. The truth is that anything good you have accomplished was through God's grace, and was usually only possible because of the help and influence of others. Practicing giving thanks in all things also helps to restore reality and a proper focus.

One reason the Lord allows testing in our lives is to show us our desperate need for Him and allow us to identify with the pain and failures of others. Mercy and humility are a byproduct of such suffering. When one sees the desperate sinfulness of one's own heart, and how God's grace makes all the difference, pride goes out the window. We need to be more thankful for the trials and tests He allows us to experience. The humility and mercy we receive (or are restored to) form the vessel into which God's grace can be poured. His grace will allow us to go on to victory and usefulness in Him.

Lord, forgive me for the pride that so often permeates my life. I realize that without You, I am nothing, a desperate failure. I know that any good thing I seem to have accomplished has only been by Your grace giving me motivation and the strength. In Your mercy You have put people in my life to motivate me and develop my character. Godly people You have sent have helped and encouraged me in every good thing I have done for You.

Thank you for the areas of weakness and testing that You, in Your wisdom, have allowed to stay in my life. These trials show me my desperate need for You and the wickedness of my old nature. Thank you for saving me and redeeming my life from destruction. I ask You, Holy Spirit, to convict me any time I listen to my old nature or the enemy, and begin to believe conceited lies about myself. I turn from such lies and acknowledge that all good things come from You, Lord. In Jesus' name I pray, Amen.

Deuteronomy 8:13, 14, 16-18: [13]...and when your herds and flocks grow large and your silver and gold increase and all you have is multiplied, [14]then your heart will become proud and you will forget the LORD your God, who brought you out of Egypt, out of the land of slavery. [16]He gave you manna to eat in the desert, something your fathers had never known, to humble and to test you so that in the end it might go well with you. [17]You may say to yourself, "My power and the strength of my hands have produced this wealth for me." [18]But remember the LORD your God, for it is he who gives you the ability to produce wealth, and so confirms his covenant, which he swore to your forefathers, as it is today. [1]

II Chronicles 7:14: [14]...if My people who are called by My name will humble themselves, and pray and seek My face, and turn from their wicked ways, then I will hear from heaven, and will forgive their sin and heal their land. [2]

II Chronicles 32:24-26: [24]In those days Hezekiah became ill and was at the point of death. He prayed to the LORD, who answered him and gave him a miraculous sign. [25]But Hezekiah's heart was proud and he did not respond to the kindness shown him; therefore the LORD'S wrath was on him and on Judah and Jerusalem. [26]Then Hezekiah repented of the pride of his heart, as did the people of Jerusalem; therefore the LORD'S wrath did not come upon them during the days of Hezekiah. [1]

Psalms 30:6: [6]Now as for me, I said in my prosperity, "I will never be moved." [7]O LORD, by Your favor You have made my mountain to stand strong; You hid Your face, I was dismayed. [3]

Job 31:24-25, 28: [24]If I have made gold my hope, or said to fine gold, "*You are* my confidence"; [25]If I have rejoiced because my wealth *was* great, and because my hand had gained much; [28]This also *would be* an iniquity *deserving of* judgment, for I would have denied God *who is* above. [2]

Psalms 37:11: [11]But the humble will inherit the land and will delight themselves in abundant prosperity. [3]

Jeremiah 9:23-24: [23]Thus says the LORD, "Let not a wise man boast of his wisdom, and let not the mighty man boast of his might, let not a rich man boast of his riches; [24]but let him who boasts boast of this, that he understands and knows Me, that I am the LORD who exercises loving kindness, justice and righteousness on earth; for I delight in these things," declares the LORD. [3]

Proverbs 11:2: [2]When pride comes, then comes disgrace, but with humility comes wisdom. [1]
Oh Father, I don't want the disgrace that pride brings. I humble myself before You. I acknowledge that any good thing I have done has been from You. Help me to glory only in that I know You, the God who delights in and exercises loving kindness, justice and right-eousness. Help me be more like You.

Proverbs 15:25: [25]The LORD will destroy the house of the proud, but He will establish the boundary of the widow. [2]

Proverbs 15:33: [33]The fear of the LORD teaches a man wisdom, and humility comes before honor. [1]

Proverbs 16:5: [5]The LORD detests all the proud of heart. Be sure of this: They will not go unpunished. [1]

Proverbs 16:18-19: [18]Pride *goes* before destruction, and a haughty spirit before a fall. [19]Better *to be* of a humble spirit with the lowly, than to divide the spoil with the proud. [2]

Proverbs 18:12: [12]Before destruction the heart of man is haughty, but humility *goes* before honor. [3] *Lord, the enemy often sings my praises to puff me up, right before he attacks. Help me to recognize his lies and false praise and to humble myself before You. Spirit of Truth, open my eyes and help me to see through his lies.*

Proverbs 22:4: [4]The reward of humility *and* the fear of the LORD are riches, honor and life. [3]

Isaiah 66:2: [2]"Has not my hand made all these things, and so they came into being?" declares the LORD. "This is the one I esteem: he who is humble and contrite in spirit, and trembles at my word." [1] *Holy Spirit, forgive me when I've not trembled at Your word, but considered my obedience to be optional. I abhor that attitude in myself and ask for Your help. I want to be Your obedient servant.*

Micah 6:8: [8]He has shown you, O man, what *is* good; and what does the LORD require of you but to do justly, to love mercy, and to walk humbly with your God? [2]

Luke 1:52-53: [52]He has brought down rulers from their thrones, but has lifted up the humble. [53]He has filled the hungry with good things, but has sent the rich away empty. [1]

Philippians 2:3-4: [3]Do nothing from selfishness or empty conceit, but with humility of mind regard one another as more important than yourselves; [4]do not *merely* look out for your own personal interests, but also for the interests of others. [3]

I Peter 5:5-6: [5]You younger men, likewise, be subject to *your* elders; and all of you, clothe yourselves with humility toward one another, for GOD IS OPPOSED TO THE PROUD, BUT GIVES GRACE TO THE HUMBLE. [6]Therefore humble yourselves under the mighty hand of God, that He may exalt you at the proper time. [1]

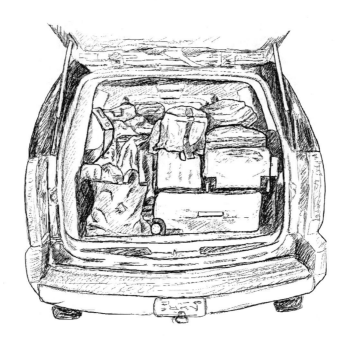

18.

PROMISES OF ABRAHAM

The New Testament tells us that in Christ we have the blessing of Abraham. The greatest of Abraham's blessings, of course, is that of receiving righteousness through faith. Yet Abraham had other blessings that we can also receive by faith. Like him, those who bless *us* will be blessed, and those who curse *us* will be cursed (Gen. 12:3). Abraham received God's favor on all he did.

One of the promises God gave Abraham was of receiving land (Gen. 13:17). Purchasing land, particularly in a new city where the Lord has sent you to minister, is a spiritually significant event, one in which the enemy may oppose you.

After getting unpacked in our rental home in Kingsport, Tennessee, one thing on my agenda was to find land. I had a long-time dream to design and build a home. I wanted a view of the nearby North Carolina Mountains, and a southern slope, with the front of the house facing north. (The direction of the desired lay of the land was for energy efficiency purposes—passive solar heating.)

We looked for over a year at both houses and land, and found nothing. One day, after seeing a beautiful house that was still not right for us, I felt something rise up in me. I asked our wonderful realtor, "Connie, are you sure there isn't any land in Sullivan County that has a view facing south?" She paused for several moments, and then remembered some land she had tried to sell several years before. She told us it had passed through the hands of nearly every realtor in town. She took us by the access road to it, but didn't know how big the land was, its price, or if it was even still for sale. It had a large hill and looked promising, and had been owned by multiple heirs of a large estate.

About two and a half weeks later, Connie faxed us a plat for the land with the asking price. That Saturday, we gathered the kids up and set out to hike the land to see if it had any view. We drove over a large hill on the way there and discovered that the haze prevented a view of the mountains. We discussed turning back, but decided to press on. We were leaving the next day to go out of town to a mountain cabin for a week's vacation.

When we approached the land, there were shirtless, sweaty men cutting large logs that were stacked around the cul-de-sac that was the access to the property. I felt a distinct prompting from the Spirit to ask one of the men if they knew anything about the land. I did and the man said that the owner and a realtor had come by the day before and asked him to remove the wood, as they were going to be putting the land up for auction on Monday (in two days). We explored the land (it seemed quite promising) and then went home, called Connie and packed for our trip.

On Sunday morning, Connie got back to us and told us that the land was indeed going to be signed over to the auctioneers the next day, and that its price would likely increase greatly as a result. Our best bet was to make an offer that day! After church, instead of heading to our mountain cabin, we drove in our fully packed SUV to where we could see the land and prayed for wisdom and God's will. On the way to work up the contract, I called my pastor and he felt good about it. He said that possessing land was a spiritually significant event for us, and that if it were him, he would not leave town until the contract was signed. (I was very sorry to hear that!)

Connie met us at McDonald's and we wrote up the contract. She told us to go ahead on our trip, as we could finish up the rest by cell phone and fax machine. I felt convicted that my pastor's advice was of the Lord. We told the kids that we felt we needed to be obedient to the word the Lord had given us, but were starting our vacation now. While eating pizza and watching a movie at home later that night, the phone rang. Connie said that they had a counter offer (which was within what we felt the land was worth). If we would come down right then, we could sign off on the contract. If not the heirs would sign it over to the auctioneers the next morning. We found ourselves at the lawyer's office at 10:30 Sunday night signing the papers!

Monday morning we headed up to the mountains to the cabin. They graciously forgave us Sunday night's rental fee. We discovered that there was no cell phone service up there. We also discovered that the building with the phone and fax machine was locked at five p.m. If we had gone on to the mountains on Sunday as our realtor advised us, we would have never gotten the land. Praise the Lord for His blessing on us, and for the word of the Lord through the man of God. God is good!

Lord, by faith, I humbly claim the blessing of Abraham. I believe you for blessings on my finances, and for possession of land according to Your plan. By faith I receive Your favor because I believe in You, obey You, and put all my trust in You. I believe You for Your favor on my descendants, and for them to become mighty in You. Most of all, I believe You for grace to please You with my life and to accomplish the destiny You have for me. In the Lord Jesus' name I ask these things, Amen.

Romans 4:16: Therefore *it is* of faith that *it might be* according to grace, so that the promise might be sure to all the seed, not only to those who are of the law, but also to those who are of the faith of Abraham, who is the father of us all. [2]

Acts 3:25: And you are heirs of the prophets and of the covenant God made with your fathers. He said to Abraham, 'Through your offspring all peoples on earth will be blessed.' [1]

Galatians 3:6: Consider Abraham: "He believed God, and it was credited to him as righteousness." [7]Understand, then, that those who believe are children of Abraham. . . [9]So those who have faith are blessed along with Abraham, the man of faith. . . [13]Christ redeemed us from the curse of the law by becoming a curse for us, for it is written: "Cursed is everyone who is hung on a tree." [14]He redeemed us in order that the blessing given to Abraham might come to the Gentiles through Christ Jesus . . . [29]If you belong to Christ, then you are Abraham's seed, and heirs according to the promise. [1]

Genesis 12:1-3: [1]Now the LORD had said to Abram: "Get out of your country, from your family and from your father's house, to a land that I will show you. [2]I will make you a great nation; I will bless you and make your name great; and you shall be a blessing. [3]I will bless those who bless you, and I will curse him who curses you; and in you all the families of the earth shall be blessed." [2]

Genesis 13:1-2: [1]So Abram went up from Egypt to the Negev, with his wife and everything he had, and Lot went with him. [2]Abram had become very wealthy in livestock and in silver and gold. [1]

Genesis 13:14, 17: [14]And the LORD said to Abram, after Lot had separated from him: "Lift your eyes now and look from the place where you are—northward, southward, eastward, and westward; . . . [17]Arise, walk in the land through its length and its width, for I give it to you." [2]

Genesis 15:1:[1]After these things the word of the LORD came to Abram in a vision, saying, "Do not be afraid, Abram. I *am* your shield, your exceedingly great reward." [2]

Lord, please be my shield and defense from man and from the enemy. Lord, knowing You, is my greatest desire and reward. Forgive me for putting idols before You.

Genesis 21:22: [22]At that time Abimelech and Phicol the commander of his forces said to Abraham, "God is with you in everything you do. [1]

Lord, please keep me from any enterprise in which You can't be with me, or from any timing of any endeavor You can't bless.

Genesis 22:15-17: [15]Then the angel of the LORD called to Abraham a second time from heaven, [16]and said, "By Myself I have sworn, declares the LORD, because you have done this thing and have not withheld your son, your only son . . . [17]indeed I will greatly bless you, and I will greatly multiply your seed as the stars of the heavens and as the sand which is on the seashore; and your seed shall possess the gate of their enemies." [3]

Lord, I give You the things most dear to me: my family, my friends and the things with which You have blessed me. Have Your way with them and with my life. I trust in You and in Your love for me. In Jesus' name I pray.

Genesis 24:35: (Abraham's servant speaking while in Aram at Bethuel and Laban's house, looking for a wife for Isaac) [35]"The LORD has greatly blessed my master, so that he has become rich; and He has given him flocks and herds, and silver and gold, and servants and maids, and camels and donkeys. [3]

Genesis 28:4: (Isaac blessing Jacob as he left to go to relatives in Aram)[4] "May he give you and your descendants the blessing given to Abraham, so that you may take possession of the land where you now live as an alien, the land God gave to Abraham." [1]

Deuteronomy 8:18: . . . [18]you shall remember the LORD your God, for *it is* He who gives you power to get wealth, that He may establish His covenant which He swore to your fathers, as *it is* this day. [2]

. . . .

Rodney's and Nita's Testimony

Even if you are in a foreign land, in a location where you know no one, **the Lord knows you** and provides for you. The following illustrations demonstrate God's faithful provision.

In July, 2007, we were in Cape Town, South Africa. One day we went sight-seeing and rode the cable car up majestic Table Mountain. As we were walking around and taking in the exhilarating view, we met a young man wearing an Auburn University sweatshirt. We found out he was an employee of the U.S. government, stationed in Saudi Arabia. His wife is South African. We chatted for a few moments and parted. Later in the restaurant he walked over to us and put a $100 bill on our table. He said that though his tithe goes to his local church, he wanted to sow some seed into our work in South Africa.

In April, 2008, driving from Johannesburg to Durban, in South Africa, Nita had voiced a desire to eat lunch at a Spur Restaurant – one of our favorites. Just as we drove into a place we had never been, the old Afrikaner town of Piet Retief (200 miles from Johannesburg), there was a Spur adjacent to a service station. As we finished lunch, a young man we had never seen before and who did not know us, approached our table. He shared with us that he is a born-again Christian and felt he was supposed to buy our lunch. He said that as he passed by us, he had sensed the presence of God. We were blessed by the fact that he gave us an amount of money more than four times the price of our meal! But the greatest blessing was that **we felt God was using this incident to confirm we were on the right path – that He knows right where we are, is with us, and intends on providing for us.**

19.

WISDOM

One of the character qualities the Holy Spirit brings to us is the desire to learn about both spiritual and natural things. Apathy for learning (in general, not just "classroom" learning) implies some serious underlying problem of the soul. Such lack of any desire for learning can spring from a false sense of superiority (haughtiness), laziness, severe fatigue or from a slumbering, wounded or grieving spirit. Remember, every person you encounter has an area of knowledge or wisdom that you can learn from, *if* you are humble enough to look for and receive it.

Early in my medical training, I heard a professor say something that made a profound impression on me. He said that as a Christian physician, I had to first of all be good at what I was doing, and then add to that compassion, integrity, spiritual strength and wisdom. If I had great compassion and spirituality, but was a poor doctor, I would ruin any witness I had as a believer and bring disgrace to the Lord's name. As a result, I made a decision to apply myself to learning all I needed to know as a physician, with all diligence, as unto the Lord. I knew He had called me, and therefore I had to be as good as I could be without compromising my faith and walk in Him. I was single and didn't have to juggle family responsibilities, but I was faithful to my local church, including a Wednesday night home group. I've never regretted the small sacrifice I made. (By the way, it was at that home group where I met my wife!)

Without wisdom and knowledge, most will probably not gain wealth. Wealth *without* wisdom will not satisfy, and probably will be quickly lost. Wisdom is worth much more than wealth or fame, because wisdom comes from the Lord and brings life. It is wisdom to obey the Lord and to be led by His Spirit. His wisdom comes only to those who seek it. There is a partial wisdom that may come to unbelievers, but it brings only a partial or superficial satisfaction, even if it brings some wealth.

Lord Jesus, give me a true hunger for wisdom, and a rightful fear of You. Convict me sorely if I begin to think myself too great to learn from those I consider lowly. Teach me true wisdom by Your Spirit so I will know how to live my life. I also need Your wisdom in order to please You, and to fulfill the destiny You have for me. I want to learn of You for my own sake. I also want to learn so that in turn, I will be able to bless others when they are hungry for understanding.

I acknowledge that only with Your timing will good come to others when I share with them. When I wait on You, and speak only by the prompting of Your Spirit, You will breathe on my words, and understanding and light will come to others' lives. Outside of Your leading and anointing, I will only pass on soulish or mental knowledge that will produce no life, but may either cause frustration and confusion, or may produce arrogance in other people.

Please bring people into my life from whom I can learn Your ways. When I pray, and read Your word, please teach me whatever I need to know. In Jesus' name I pray, Amen.

Proverbs 1:7: [7]The fear of the LORD *is* the beginning of knowledge, *but* fools despise wisdom and instruction. [2]

Proverbs 3:13-19: [13]Blessed is the man who finds wisdom, the man who gains understanding, [14]for she is more profitable than silver and yields better returns than gold. [15]She is more precious than rubies; nothing you desire can compare with her. [16]Long life is in her right hand; in her left hand are riches and honor. [17]Her ways are pleasant ways, and all her paths are peace. [18]She is a tree of life to those who embrace her; those who lay hold of her will be blessed. [19]By wisdom the LORD laid the earth's foundations, by understanding he set the heavens in place; [1]

Proverbs 14:18: [18]The naive inherit folly, but the prudent are crowned with knowledge. [3/1]

Proverbs 16:16: [16]How much better it is to get wisdom than gold! And to get understanding is to be chosen above silver. [3]

Job 28:15-19: [15]It cannot be bought with the finest gold, nor can its price be weighed in silver. [16]It cannot be bought with the gold of Ophir, with precious onyx or sapphires. [17]Neither gold nor crystal can compare with it, nor can it be had for jewels of gold. [18]Coral and jasper are not worthy of mention; the price of wisdom is beyond rubies. [19]The topaz of Cush cannot compare with it; it cannot be bought with pure gold. [1]

Proverbs 20:15: [15]There is gold, and an abundance of jewels; but the lips of knowledge are a more precious thing. [3]

Proverbs 24:3-4: [3]By wisdom a house is built, and through understanding it is established; [4]through knowledge its rooms are filled with rare and beautiful treasures. [1]
Holy Spirit, please give me wisdom to build my house — my family, business and ministry.

Proverbs 29:3: [3]A man who loves wisdom brings joy to his father, but a companion of prostitutes squanders his wealth. [1]

Ecclesiastes 4:13: [13]A poor yet wise lad is better than an old and foolish king who no longer knows *how* to receive instruction. [3]

James 3:17: [17]But the wisdom from above is first pure, then peaceable, gentle, reasonable, full of mercy and good fruits, unwavering, without hypocrisy. [3]

20.

PROTECTION

Protection and safety are a part of our heritage in Christ. Both are part of the meaning of the Greek word *soteria,* which is usually translated "salvation". Without safety and shelter from harm, prosperity is of no value and actually is not even possible. Fortunately, the Lord has promised us total security in Him, but as everything else in our Christian lives, it must be received by faith. Let the following scriptures fortify your soul and spirit for tough times when fear would try and overtake you. I would also highly recommend meditation on a tiny, wonderful book by Gloria Copeland called "Promise of Protection". It is a great well digger and will form a great refuge of strength in your life! Although this little book is currently out of print, you can probably find it on line.

I have read "Promise of Protection" (formerly "Build Yourself an Ark") regularly as part of my well digging. I now read it through a few times each year, reading a chapter a day as part of my devotions. When 9/11 happened, I confessed repeatedly, "The Lord is my stronghold; I will not be afraid. I will trust in Him, and He will deliver me. Though a thousand fall at my side, and ten thousand at my right hand, it will not come near me." I had peace through it all, and was initially surprised to see how afraid some people were around me. People asked me why I had no fear, and I simply told them that I knew the Lord would take care of me, and told them about the book. I realized that the Lord had done a work in my heart, and that I had dug at least a small well of faith for God's protection.

Our oldest child, Sarah, was born prematurely, at about six month's gestation (27 weeks out of the normal 40 week pregnancy). She weighed 1 lb. 10 oz. and was 12 inches long! She had to have several surgeries and nearly died once. Not only were we praying for her, but people from our church came daily and prayed outside the window that was next to her bed. The nurses of the neonatal intensive care unit (NICU) were impressed.

One thing we prayed for regularly was for the Lord to put angels around Sarah's bed, but we didn't think a whole lot about it. We got to know other parents and grandparents of the babies there, particularly a grandmother and great-grandmother of a little girl named Brandy. Brandy was very sick and they said her brain was like Swiss cheese (full of holes). The NICU's goal was to get Brandy to the point that they didn't have to call a code for her (for resuscitation) for enough days in a row so they could send her home where they knew she would die, but at least in dignity.

After Sarah's first three weeks in the NICU she was moved to a slightly less sick aisle and was put right beside Brandy. One day as we were spending time with Brandy's grandmother at the bedsides of Sarah and Brandy, she noted that Brandy seemed to be doing much better. She had needed resuscitation several times a day, but recently hadn't needed it for a couple of days. The nurses and doctors began talking about sending Brandy home soon.

Sarah continued to improve and was finally strong enough to be transferred to the next aisle over. When she did, Brandy took a sudden turn for the worse. Her poor grandmother and great-grandmother were discouraged. We realized one day that the Lord had put strong warrior angels by Sarah's bed with flaming swords. They moved with Sarah. When Sarah was moved to be right by Brandy, Brandy was protected and strengthened by their presence, but now Sarah (and her angels) had left. We praised God (while grieving for our friends), knowing that the heavenly host (angels) were protecting Sarah, even when we could not be there for her. God is good!

Lord, I thank you for promising me protection from harm under every circumstance. Forgive me for times when I have allowed fear to overcome me, instead of looking to You. You are my strong fortress and my high tower in a time of war, and my refuge from every storm. When trouble comes, I will not give way to fear, but I will put my trust in You. Your right arm will uphold me. Every plan of the enemy to hurt me will fail, because I am the apple of Your eye. My mouth will speak of Your salvation from danger. You are my peace and I trust You to save me, in Jesus' name, Amen.

Leviticus 26: 3, 6-10: [3]If you walk in My statutes and keep My commandments so as to carry them out, [6]I shall also grant peace in the land, so that you may lie down with no one making you tremble. I shall also eliminate harmful beasts from the land, and no sword will pass through your land. [7]But you will chase your enemies and they will fall before you by the sword; [8]five of you will chase a hundred, and a hundred of you will chase ten thousand, and your enemies will fall before you by the sword. [9]So I will turn toward you and make you fruitful and multiply you, and I will confirm My covenant with you. [10]You will eat the old supply and clear out the old because of the new. [3]

Deuteronomy 28:1, 7: [1]Now it shall come to pass, if you diligently obey the voice of the LORD your God, to observe carefully all His commandments which I command you today, that the LORD your

God will set you high above all nations of the earth. . .[7]The LORD will cause your enemies who rise against you to be defeated before your face; they shall come out against you one way and flee before you seven ways. [3]

I Chronicles 16:21-23: [21]He permitted no man to oppress them, and He reproved kings for their sakes, *saying,* [22]"Do not touch My anointed ones, and do My prophets no harm." [23]Sing to the LORD, all the earth; proclaim good tidings of His salvation from day to day. [3]

Job 5:17-21: [17]Behold, happy *is* the man whom God corrects; therefore do not despise the chastening of the Almighty. [18]For He bruises, but He binds up; He wounds, but His hands make whole. [19]He shall deliver you in six troubles, yes, in seven no evil shall touch you. [20]In famine He shall redeem you from death, and in war from the power of the sword. [21]You shall be hidden from the scourge of the tongue, and you shall not be afraid of destruction when it comes. [2]

Psalms 27:1-6: [1]The LORD is my light and my salvation - whom shall I fear? The LORD is the stronghold of my life - of whom shall I be afraid? [2]When evil men advance against me to devour my flesh, when my enemies and my foes attack me, they will stumble and fall. [3]Though an army besiege me, my heart will not fear; though war break out against me, even then will I be confident. [4]One thing I ask of the LORD, this is what I seek: that I may dwell in the house of the LORD all the days of my life, to gaze upon the beauty of the LORD and to seek him in his temple. [5]For in the day of trouble he will keep me safe in his dwelling; he will hide me in the shelter of his tabernacle and set me high upon a rock. [6]Then my head will be exalted above the enemies who surround me; at his tabernacle will I sacrifice with shouts of joy; I will sing and make music to the LORD. [1]

Psalms 33:16-22: [16]No king is saved by the size of his army; no warrior escapes by his great strength. [17]A horse is a vain hope for deliverance; despite all its great strength it cannot save. [18]But the eyes of the LORD are on those who fear him, on those whose hope is in his unfailing love, [19]to deliver them from death and keep them alive in famine. [20]We wait in hope for the LORD; he is our help and our shield. [21]In him our hearts rejoice, for we trust in his holy name. [22]May your unfailing love rest upon us, O LORD, even as we put our hope in you. [1]

Psalms 91: [1]He who dwells in the secret place of the Most High shall abide under the shadow of the Almighty. [2]I will say of the LORD, "*He is* my refuge and my fortress; My God, in Him I will trust." [3]Surely He shall deliver you from the snare of the fowler *and* from the perilous pestilence. [4]He shall cover you with His feathers, and under His wings you shall take refuge; His truth *shall be your* shield and buckler. [5]You shall not be afraid of the terror by night, *nor* of the arrow *that* flies by day, [6]*Nor* of the pestilence *that* walks in darkness, *nor* of the destruction *that* lays waste at noonday. [7]A thousand may fall at your side, and ten thousand at your right hand; *but* it shall not come near you. [8]Only with your eyes shall you look, and see the reward of the wicked. [9]Because you have made the LORD, *who is* my refuge, *even* the Most High, your dwelling place, [10]No evil shall befall you, nor shall any plague come near your dwelling; [11]For He shall give His angels charge over you, to keep you in all your ways. [12]In *their* hands they shall bear you up, lest you dash your foot against a stone. [13]You shall tread upon the lion and the cobra, the young lion and the serpent you shall trample underfoot. [14]"Because he has set his love upon Me, therefore I will deliver him; I will set him on high, because he has known My name. [15]He shall call upon Me, and I will answer him; I *will be* with him in trouble; I will deliver him and honor him. [16]With long life I will satisfy him, and show him My salvation. [2]

22 ACRES, MILLEDGEVILLE, GA

21.

CONDITIONS (PART II)

The old covenant (of Moses) was based on law. Follow the law and you are blessed; disobey and be cursed. The new covenant is based on faith; by faith we are heirs of Christ and partakers of His promises. Yet even in the New Testament, many (if not most) promises are conditional. Furthermore, Paul makes it clear (see Romans 8:2-13) that only as we walk in the Spirit will we fulfill our destiny in Christ and receive everything He has planned for us. Christ bore the curse of sin for us, yet in Gal. 6:7 Paul says, "Do not be deceived, God is not mocked; for whatever a man sows, that he will also reap." So there are natural and spiritual consequences for what we do, both for good and for evil. Actually, the majority of the promises in the Old Testament apply today. The difference is that obedience *then* was to the law, and *now* is to the "law of the Spirit of life in Christ Jesus" (Rom. 8:2). In both cases the Lord wanted (wants) obedience from the heart out of relationship. The Lord desires good for us, so let us press on to seek and obey Him.

During the first month or so of my unemployment, an opportunity came open for our church to buy 22 wonderful acres of land for a great price right on the bypass highway around the town. It was a perfect location and we desperately needed room to expand. The only catch was that we needed to get the money together in eight days. If we failed to come up with the finances, it would pass on to one of several other buyers who were waiting with better offers. We were exhorted by the pastor to pray about what we should give.

God had blessed me in the previous few months just before I left the hospital and we had considerably more savings than usual, for which I was grateful and in which I took a little comfort. As I prayed, I was keenly aware of our insecure (potentially dire) financial position, and imagined our gift towards the land would be less generous than it might have been under other circumstances. When the Lord prompted me with an amount, I almost gasped, as it was a quarter of our savings. I argued for a moment with God, but that got me nowhere. Then I asked my wife if she could confirm what I was hearing. I secretly expected her to say that I was being ridiculous, and then I would breathe a sigh of relief, since we would want to agree on any decision that huge. Instead, she took a deep breath and said that it was probably God!

As I grappled with the idea, I realized that I needed God's blessing on my finances more than the finances themselves. Any amount of money would eventually run out, but God's provision would endure. We were obedient, and I never regretted it. I believe that the seed we sowed in obedience is part of what kept us those three years. We made mistakes in our finances and yet the Lord was merciful and upheld us. Praise the Lord! It is a good thing to obey Him.

Lord, I want to follow You with all my heart. I thank You for all Your provision for me and that You want to bless me. Holy Spirit, convict of me of anything in my life that displeases You, or stops Your hand of blessing on my life. Lord, as I read these scriptures, show me what You want to change in me, and how I should make the changes You desire for me. Help me to treat others the way I want You to treat me. I love you. In Jesus' name I pray, Amen.

Matthew 19:29: 29And everyone who has left houses or brothers or sisters or father or mother or children or farms for My name's sake, will receive many times as much, and will inherit eternal life. 3

Matthew 25:45-47: 45Who then is the faithful and wise servant, whom the master has put in charge of the servants in his household to give them their food at the proper time? 46It will be good for that servant whose master finds him doing so when he returns. 47I tell you the truth, he will put him in charge of all his possessions. 1

Deuteronomy 30:8-10: 8You will again obey the LORD and follow all his commands I am giving you today. 9Then the LORD your God will make you most prosperous in all the work of your hands and in the fruit of your womb, the young of your livestock and the crops of your land. The LORD will again delight in you and make you prosperous, just as he delighted in your fathers, 10if you obey the LORD your God and keep his commands and decrees that are written in this Book of the Law and turn to the LORD your God with all your heart and with all your soul. 1

Isaiah 1:19: 19"If you are willing and obedient, you will eat the best from the land; 20but if you resist and rebel, you will be devoured by the sword." For the mouth of the LORD has spoken. 1

Jeremiah 17:9-10: 9The heart is deceitful above all things and beyond cure. Who can understand it? 10I the LORD search the heart and examine the mind, to reward a man according to his conduct, according to what his deeds deserve. 1

Deuteronomy 30:15-17: 15See, I set before you today life and prosperity, death and destruction. 16For I command you today to love the LORD your God, to walk in his ways, and to keep his commands, decrees and laws; then you will live and increase, and the LORD your God will bless you in the land you are entering to possess. [17]But if your heart turns away and you are not obedient, and if you are drawn away to bow down to other gods and worship them, [18]I declare to you this day that you will certainly be destroyed. You will not live long in the land you are crossing the Jordan to enter and possess. [1]

Deuteronomy 30:19-20: [19]I call heaven and earth to witness against you today, that I have set before you life and death, the blessing and the curse. So choose life in order that you may live, you and your descendants, [20]by loving the LORD your God, by obeying His voice, and by holding fast to Him; for this is your life and the length of your days, that you may live in the land which the LORD swore to your fathers, to Abraham, Isaac, and Jacob, to give them. [3]

Deuteronomy 7:12: [2]"Then it shall come about, because you *listen to these judgments and keep and do them*, that the LORD your God will keep with you His covenant and His loving kindness which He swore to your forefathers. [13]He will love you and bless you and multiply you; He will also bless the fruit of your womb and the fruit of your ground, your grain and your new wine and your oil, the increase of your herd and the young of your flock, in the land which He swore to your forefathers to give you. [14]You shall be blessed above all peoples; there will be no male or female barren among you or among your cattle. [15]The LORD will remove from you all sickness; and He will not put on you any of the harmful diseases of Egypt which you have known, but He will lay them on all who hate you. [3]

Proverbs 14:24: [24]The crown of the wise is their riches, *but* the foolishness of fools *is* folly. [2]

Proverbs 22:4: [4]The reward of humility *and* the fear of the LORD are riches, honor and life.[3]

Deuteronomy 5:29: [9]Oh, that their hearts would be inclined to fear me and keep all my commands always, so that it might go well with them and their children forever! [1]

Lord help me to always walk in reverent fear of You.

Proverbs 28:13: [13]He who conceals his transgressions will not prosper, but he who confesses and forsakes *them* will find compassion. [3]

Deuteronomy 12:28: [8]Observe and obey all these words which I command you, that it may go well with you and your children after you forever, when you do *what is* good and right in the sight of the LORD your God. [2]

Proverbs 28:19,20 : [9]He who tills his land will have plenty of bread, but he who follows frivolity will have poverty enough! [20]A faithful man will abound with blessings, but he who hastens to be rich will not go unpunished. [2]

Lord, show me where I've followed frivolity instead of being faithful. Show me when to work and when to play. If the love of money has made me long for get rich quick schemes, please convict me so the enemy can't take advantage of my idolatry.

· · · · · · · · · · ·

Linda's Testimony
Part 2

In the year 2000, I was offered a rental proposition that turned into a great blessing from the Lord. I was renting a small framed house for $300 a month. I had learned in a Bill Gothard seminar as a very young Christian that I should take care of rental property like it was my own. So I carpeted and painted and did other extras at my own expense. A friend approached me and asked if I wanted to rent her house for the same amount that I was paying. I began to pray about it and the Lord said to take it. I did the same thing with that house. A close friend came and we painted the entire house. It was a brick house, much nicer than the framed one.

About a year later I decided I would buy the house and God told me the house would be a blessing. While we were getting the paperwork in order, a sibling died and it stopped all the procedures, because the house was part of an estate. The attorney called me and said not to pay any rent until new papers were drawn up. That turn of events provided almost a year of free rent! God rewarded my sowing with a much bigger harvest. Now I am **buying** the house. To God be the glory!

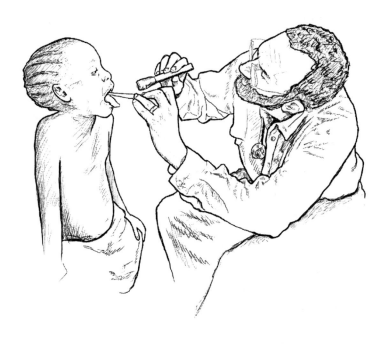

22.

DEUTERONOMY 28

I believe that the promises in Deuteronomy 28 are available to us. The promises are conditional on obeying the law. We are no longer under the law of Moses, but we are under the law of the Spirit. The law says: "Do not commit adultery." The law of the Spirit says: "Do not even look at a woman to lust after her." We are not getting off easy, but we have the power of the Holy Spirit to help us. We also have the blood of Jesus covering us, the very righteousness of Christ. We are in Him, and He obeyed the law perfectly. If I am intentionally disobeying things I know the Lord has told me, I won't have confidence to claim and receive these things. But if I am right with the Lord, confessing my sins and turning from them, and if I am pressing on to obey what He has told me to do, then I will have confidence to come before Him. Then I can receive everything He has for me.

Early in my family practice internship, before we had any children, I had a slow evening while I was on call in the hospital. I had a several hour conversation with my wife and we talked about our dreams. One such dream was for us to do a three-month rotation of my residency on the mission field. We believed it was of the Lord and prayed over the telephone that the Lord would show the way and provide all the finances abundantly.

After Sarah was born prematurely, I was asked to speak for a Full Gospel Businessmen's Fellowship luncheon meeting. I had a divine encounter with a man sitting next to me. He worked for a Christian drug company. They were looking to get some research projects done overseas, and I fit the bill. It was arranged that I would do advance research, and then travel with a pathologist who would supervise me to validate the project. They paid me well for the time I spent doing research in advance. They bought a portable crib for our then nine-month-old Sarah, as well as enough dehydrated supplemental baby food to last her three months. They even bought us nice suitcases, since we could not afford luggage that would stand up to rigors of overseas travel.

Three days before we were to leave, the pathologist who was going to travel with me became unable to go. The next day, the drug company decided to pull funding for the trip. We prayed hard on hearing the news. First my wife, and then I, realized that the Lord had told us to go and that He would provide the money with or without the drug company. I made several calls, by the prompting of the Lord, and through His people, God provided enough to cover the trip. We were even able to keep all the things the drug company had purchased us for the trip.

The trip was a wonderful success, both professionally and spiritually. We spent three months in Addis Ababa, capital of (then Marxist) Ethiopia. My sister and brother-in-law were Baptist missionaries there at the time and helped us with housing and transportation. I worked at the large teaching hospital in town and saw fantastic cases that are common there, but rare in this country. I was able to take the medical school parasitology class and lab at no charge. I had my guitar and was able to minister by leading worship for the missionaries and also at the English-speaking church they were attending. We even got to help a beginning underground church! God used Sarah, who was already blind, and through her He broke down walls of prejudice against us. Before we came back we sold all my textbooks and the portable crib to Ethiopians, who were thrilled to get them. Truly we were blessed going out and coming in. We lacked finances, not only for the airline tickets, but even for luggage and supplies for Sarah, but God provided it all for us. He is so good.

Lord, I love You and belong to You. Everything I have belongs to You, and I am pressing on to fulfill Your call on my life. I thank you that I am blessed coming in and going out. Thank you for making me the head and not the tail (Deut. 28:13), and for prospering the works of my hands. I believe You to make me one who can play a part of financing the Kingdom of God. In Jesus' name I pray, Amen.

Deuteronomy 28:1-14: [1]Now it shall come to pass, if you diligently obey the voice of the LORD your God, to observe carefully all His commandments which I command you today, that the LORD your God will set you high above all nations of the earth. [2]And all these blessings shall come upon you and overtake you, because you obey the voice of the LORD your God: [3]Blessed *shall* you *be* in the city, and blessed *shall* you *be* in the country. [4]Blessed *shall be* the fruit of your body, the produce of your ground and the increase of your herds, the increase of your cattle and the offspring of your flocks. [5]Blessed *shall be* your basket and your kneading bowl. [6]Blessed *shall* you *be* when you come in, and blessed *shall* you *be* when you go out.
[7]The LORD will cause your enemies who rise against you to be defeated before your face; they shall come out against you one way and flee before you seven ways. [8]The LORD will command the blessing on you in your storehouses and in all to which you set your hand, and He will bless you in the land which the LORD your God is giving you. [9]The LORD will establish you as a holy people to Himself, just as He has sworn to you, if you keep the commandments of the LORD your God and walk in His ways. [10]Then all peoples of

the earth shall see that you are called by the name of the LORD, and they shall be afraid of you. [11]And the LORD will grant you plenty of goods, in the fruit of your body, in the increase of your livestock, and in the produce of your ground, in the land of which the LORD swore to your fathers to give you. [12]The LORD will open to you His good treasure, the heavens, to give the rain to your land in its season, and to bless all the work of your hand. You shall lend to many nations, but you shall not borrow. [13]And the LORD will make you the head and not the tail; you shall be above only, and not be beneath, if you heed the commandments of the LORD your God, which I command you today, and are careful to observe *them*. [14]So you shall not turn aside from any of the words which I command you this day, *to* the right or the left, to go after other gods to serve them. [2]

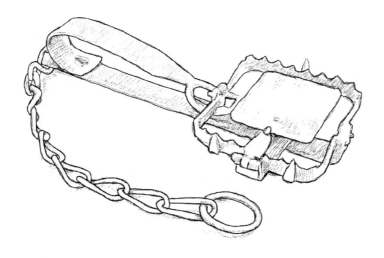

23.

WARNINGS

The enemy has many traps that are designed to delay or block the prosperity that the Lord intends for us. Search your heart and ask the Holy Spirit to shine a light on your life as you read these scriptures. Do you take home company supplies, fudge on your income taxes, or neglect to tithe? These are all forms of stealing and if you steal, then the law of sowing and reaping gives the enemy license to steal (or bring in others to steal) from you. If you are consistently, deliberately disobedient to the Lord or sell yourself to do evil, He cannot bless you. Beware of greed and putting your trust in what money can buy, as the Lord is looking to bless those who put their whole trust in Him.

As a young man, I distinctly remember a time when I was sorely tempted to buy a pornographic magazine. The Holy Spirit immediately spoke to me that buying that magazine would be taking money He had given me and turning it over to finance the kingdom of darkness. I instantly knew that if I bought the magazine, He would have to remove His blessing from my finances. It wasn't worth *that* price (and never has been).

*Lord, help me to have true wisdom in living my life so that I can please You. I know You desire to bless me and enable me to be a blessing. Show me how I have compromised myself and blocked Your hand in my life or opened the door for the devourer. Teach me to recognize the traps the enemy has for me, and show me where I need to repent. If I have ever judged wealthy or poor people, or been prejudiced against them for their prosperity or poverty, remind me so I can repent and not have to reap from it. I know that my efforts will never be enough, but I believe that You, who have begun a good work in me, **will** carry it on to completion until the day of Christ Jesus (Phil. 1:6). In His name I pray, Amen!*

Leviticus 19:11: [11]You shall not steal, nor deal falsely, nor lie to one another. [3]

Matthew 7:1, 2: [1]Do not judge, or you too will be judged. [2]For in the same way you judge others, you will be judged, and with the measure you use, it will be measured to you. [1]

Proverbs 10:9: [9]The man of integrity walks securely, but he who takes crooked paths will be found out. [1]

I Corinthians 6:10: [10]…nor thieves nor the greedy nor drunkards nor slanderers nor swindlers will inherit the kingdom of God. [1]

Romans 6:23: [23]For the wages of sin is death, but the free gift of God is eternal life in Christ Jesus our Lord. [3]

Psalms 37:37-8: [37]Consider the blameless, observe the upright; there is a future for the man of peace. [38]But all sinners will be destroyed; the future of the wicked will be cut off. [1]

II Chronicles 16:7-9: 7And at that time Hanani the seer came to Asa, King of Judah, and said to him: "Because you have relied on the King of Syria, and have not relied on the LORD your God, therefore the army of the King of Syria has escaped from your hand. 8Were the Ethiopians and the Lubim not a huge army with very many chariots and horsemen? Yet, because you relied on the LORD, He delivered them into your hand. 9For the eyes of the LORD run to and fro throughout the whole earth, to show Himself strong on behalf of *those* whose heart *is* loyal to Him. In this you have done foolishly; therefore from now on you shall have wars." 2

Deuteronomy 21:25: 25There was never a man like Ahab, who sold himself to do evil in the eyes of the Lord, urged on by Jezebel, his wife. 1

Dear Holy Spirit, please convict me where I've compromised your best for finances, convenience, pleasure or prestige. I want to stay on the narrow path and fulfill the destiny You have for my life.

Psalms 73:2, 3, 16-20, 23-26: 2But as for me, my feet had almost slipped; I had nearly lost my foothold. 3For I envied the arrogant when I saw the prosperity of the wicked. . . . 16When I tried to understand all this, it was oppressive to me 17till I entered the sanctuary of God; then I understood their final destiny. 18Surely you place them on slippery ground; you cast them down to ruin. 19How suddenly are they destroyed, completely swept away by terrors! 20As a dream when one awakes, so when you arise, O Lord, you will despise them as fantasies. 23Yet I am always with you; you hold me by my right hand. 24You guide me with your counsel, and afterward you will take me into glory. 25Whom have I in heaven but you? And earth has nothing I desire besides you. 26My flesh and my heart may fail, but God is the strength of my heart and my portion forever. 1

Proverbs 15:27: 27He who profits illicitly troubles his own house, but he who hates bribes will live. 3

Proverbs 23:4-8: 4Do not wear yourself out to get rich; have the wisdom to show restraint. 5Cast but a glance at riches, and they are gone, for they will surely sprout wings and fly off to the sky like an eagle. 6Do not eat the food of a stingy man, do not crave his delicacies; 7for he is the kind of man who is always thinking about the cost. "Eat and drink," he says to you, but his heart is not with you. [8]You will vomit up the little you have eaten and will have wasted your compliments. [1]

Proverbs 28:22: [22]A man with an evil (*and* covetous) eye hastens after riches, and does not consider that poverty will come upon him. [2] ([5])

Jeremiah 22:21-2: [21]I spoke to you in your prosperity; but you said, 'I will not listen!' This has been your practice from your youth, that you have not obeyed My voice. [22]The wind will sweep away all your shepherds, and your lovers will go into captivity; you will surely be ashamed and humiliated because of all your wickedness. [3]
Lord, forgive me for the stubbornness I've had in my life towards You in certain areas. I've refused to respond to Your conviction, closing My ears and telling myself it wasn't really You speaking. I didn't want to obey, but I also didn't want my rebellion exposed. Lord, I turn to You and ask for help. Give me a spirit of repentance and a yielded will. I choose to turn and obey You, even though it requires hard choices. Show me the real consequences of disobedience so I will choose life and not death. Help me Lord to stay completely true to You. In Jesus' name I pray, Amen.

Jeremiah 17:10-11: [10]I, the LORD, search the heart, I test the mind, even to give to each man according to his ways, according to the results of his deeds. [11]As a partridge that hatches eggs which it has not laid, *so* is he who makes a fortune, but unjustly; In the midst of his days it will forsake him, and in the end he will be a fool.[3]

Luke 12:15: [15]Then He said to them, "Beware, and be on your guard against every form of greed; for not *even* when one has an abundance does his life consist of his possessions." [3]

24.

COMMITMENT

One of the requirements God has for us in order to receive His full blessings is that we commit ourselves, and everything He has given us, to Him (2 Chron. 16:9). Faithfulness is a byproduct of commitment and is required to inherit many of the blessings He has for us. He calls us to be faithful to Him, and also to the local church and the people He puts in our lives. Through years of faithfulness, others see the real Jesus in us and come to trust us and then to trust our God.

The job in Georgia was our first experience with my being self-employed. At the end of the year we discovered, to my chagrin, that I had not put enough money aside for taxes. We fixed the problem for the coming year, and although I got a significant raise, we seemed to always be short of funds and had to postpone nearly all major purchases and many small ones. We had convictions about not going into debt for automobiles. I was driving a Yugo (with A/C and cruise control). My wife was driving a very old sedan, with 165,000 miles on it, which needed body work.

My pastor went with me to a worship seminar. On the way back from the conference (in the Yugo) I told him that my wife really wanted a minivan, but that we didn't have nearly enough saved for one. It was troubling me. He told me that he felt strongly that I ought to get her what she wanted even if it meant going into debt. I heard his counsel, but I really grappled with the dilemma it put me in. On one hand I really believed in obeying the word of the Lord from my pastor, but on the other hand the Lord had given us strong convictions about not going into debt. I cried out to God for help, for a miracle.

A few days later, Martha called me at work from a Huddle House. She had been driving with the kids and had rear-ended another vehicle (which was even older than ours) and was stranded. No one was hurt, including the other driver (praise the Lord!), and the other car was untouched (praise the Lord again!), but our vehicle was history! We prayed even harder.

It was tax time and the next day Martha finished the taxes. She called me excitedly. Apparently, I had grossly overestimated how much we needed to put aside each month for taxes. The reason we had felt so financially strapped all year was because I had instituted an enforced rigorous monthly savings plan! The rest of the story is too long to put here, but through a series of small and not so small miracles, we were able to buy a minivan without debt, even one with an extended body length, which we really needed. We had to put $1,000 on our credit card for the down payment because we were using a national buying service. We had the rest of the money because of what we had saved for the car and the extra tax money. Then the Lord brought in an unexpected extra $1,000 of income in time to pay off the credit card. So while we were committed to the convictions God had given (or perhaps because we were committed), the Lord used our pastor and sovereignly provided my wife's heart's desire. He allowed me to be obedient to the authority He placed in my life, and yet not compromise the convictions He had given us. He is very good and faithful!

Lord, I commit myself to You, anew today. I give you all that I am and have, and all I hope to do. I choose to seek You first with my life, and never put the things I want before You. I believe that You know what is best for me and want to bless me. Only You know what I can handle and what I really need. Make me a faithful servant of Yourself, one known to others by my consistency. Cause me to be a person of my word who can always be counted on. Make my life a delight to You and a blessing to those around me. In Jesus' name I pray, Amen.

Psalms 37:4-6: 4Delight yourself in the LORD and he will give you the desires of your heart. 5Commit your way to the LORD; trust in him and he will do this: 6He will make your righteousness shine like the dawn, the justice of your cause like the noonday sun. 1

Proverbs 3:5-6: 5Trust in the LORD with all your heart, and lean not on your own understanding; 6In **all** your ways acknowledge Him, and He shall direct your paths. 2

Matthew 6:33-34: 33But seek first his kingdom and his righteousness, and all these things will be given to you as well. 34Therefore, do not worry about tomorrow, for tomorrow will worry about itself. Each day has enough trouble of its own. 1

Lord, if I am really committed to You, I'll seek You first. Show me things I do that put other people and things before You. Holy Spirit, please convict me of any activity that turns my heart from having You first.

Matthew 19:27-29: 27Peter answered him, "We have left everything to follow you! What then will there be for us?" 28Jesus said to them, "I tell you the truth. . . 29And everyone who has left houses or brothers or sisters or father or mother or children or fields for my sake will receive a hundred times as much and will inherit eternal life." 1

Luke 16:10,13: [10]Whoever can be trusted with very little can also be trusted with much, and whoever is dishonest with very little will also be dishonest with much. . . [13]No servant can serve two masters. Either he will hate the one and love the other, or he will be devoted to the one and despise the other. You cannot serve both God and money." [1]

Philippians 3:8: [8]More than that, I count all things to be loss in view of the surpassing value of knowing Christ Jesus my Lord, for whom I have suffered the loss of all things, and count them but rubbish so that I may gain Christ, [3]

James 1:2-4, 22: [2]My brethren, count it all joy when you fall into various trials, [3]knowing that the testing of your faith produces patience. [4]But let patience have *its* perfect work, that you may be perfect and complete, lacking nothing. . . [22]But be doers of the word, and not hearers only, deceiving yourselves. [2]

I Peter 1:14-15: [14]As obedient children, do not conform to the evil desires you had when you lived in ignorance. [15]But just as he who called you is holy, so be holy in all you do; [1]

I John 2:17: [17]The world is passing away, and *also* its lusts; but the one who does the will of God lives forever. [3]

I John 3:22: [22]...and receive from Him anything we ask, because we obey His commands and do what pleases Him. [1]

25.

HELPING THE POOR

Helping the poor is not always emphasized in churches, but it is well taught in the scriptures. The Lord tells us that when we help the poor, it is a loan to Him, and He will repay us. There is a blessing promised on those who are considerate of others less fortunate than themselves. Jesus says that when He separates the sheep from the goats, one criterion will be what they did to Him as the "least of these," when He was hungry, thirsty, in prison or naked (Matt. 25:31-46). Part of Job's righteousness was that he helped the homeless and those who needed food or clothing. Paul was eager to help the poor. By contrast, those who take **no** pity or thought for the poor were questioned as to whether the love of God lived in their hearts.

Indeed, Sodom's sin (in Ezekiel 16:48-49) is listed as arrogance, living at ease, and not helping the poor and needy. That's company I don't want to keep! God loves to bless us, but we are not to clutch our blessing at others' expense. Rather, we trust that as the Spirit pours out compassion in our hearts and we give to others, the Lord will repay us and bless us.

Lord, forgive me for when I've not had compassion on others less fortunate than myself. I've tended to isolate myself and stop up my ears. Please forgive me and soften my heart with your convicting power. Give me ears that are quick to hear when you want me to be Your hands to bless others. Help me to unstop my ears to the cries of the needy in my neighborhood and city. Let me instead be like the Good Samaritan, and take care of the neighbors you bring my way. Help me also to learn the difference between Your compassion and mine, between Your love and my guilt. I want to obey Your Spirit and go where You are going. I pray this in Jesus' name, Amen.

Ezekiel 16:48-49: ⁴⁸"As I live," declares the Lord GOD, "Sodom, your sister and her daughters have not done as you and your daughters have done. ⁴⁹Behold, this was the guilt of your sister Sodom: she and her daughters had arrogance, abundant food and careless ease, but *she did not help the poor and needy*." ³

Father, help me remember when I feel poor, that I am tremendously well off compared to most of the world. Help me not to sin the sin of Sodom and neglect the poor and needy in my concern for myself.

Psalms 41:1: ¹Blessed *is* he who considers the poor; the LORD will deliver him in time of trouble. ²The LORD will preserve him and keep him alive, *and* he will be blessed on the earth; You will not deliver him to the will of his enemies. ³The LORD will strengthen him on his bed of illness; You will sustain him on his sickbed. ²

Leviticus 25:35-38: ³⁵If one of your countrymen becomes poor and is unable to support himself among you, help him as you would an alien or a temporary resident, so he can continue to live among you. ³⁶Do not take interest of any kind from him, but fear your God, so that your countryman may continue to live among you. ³⁷You must not lend him money at interest or sell him food at a profit. [38]I am the LORD your God, who brought you out of Egypt to give you the land of Canaan and to be your God. [1]

Proverbs 14:31: He who oppresses the poor shows contempt for their Maker, but whoever is kind to the needy honors God. [1]

Proverbs 31:20: [20]She extends her hand to the poor, yes, she reaches out her hands to the needy.[3]

Isaiah 58:6-9: [6]Is not this the kind of fasting I have chosen: to loose the chains of injustice and untie the cords of the yoke, to set the oppressed free and break every yoke? [7]**Is it not to share your food with the hungry and to provide the poor wanderer with shelter— when you see the naked, to clothe him, and not to turn away from your own flesh and blood?** [8]Then your light will break forth like the dawn, and your healing will quickly appear; then your righteousness will go before you, and the glory of the LORD will be your rear guard. [9]Then you will call, and the LORD will answer; you will cry for help, and he will say: Here am I. [1]

Daniel 4:27: [27]Therefore, O king, may my advice be pleasing to you: break away now from your sins by *doing* righteousness and from your iniquities by showing mercy to *the* poor, in case there may be a prolonging of your prosperity. [3]

Holy Spirit, show me how I should be showing mercy to the poor. Convict me and give me Your wisdom.

Matthew 6:2-4: [2]So when you give to the poor, do not sound a trumpet before you, as the hypocrites do in the synagogues and in the streets, so that they may be honored by men. Truly I say to you, they have their reward in full. [3]But when you give to the poor, do not let your left hand know what your right hand is doing, [4]so that your giving will be in secret; and your Father who sees *what is done* in secret will reward you.[3]

Proverbs 19:17: [17]He who has pity on the poor lends to the LORD, and He will pay back what he has given. [2]

Lord Jesus, when I am in need, I ask You to remember what I have given to others who were in need, and I ask You to meet my need.

Proverbs 28:8: [8]He who increases his wealth by exorbitant interest amasses it for another, who will be kind to the poor. [1]

Proverbs 28:27: [27]He who gives to the poor will lack nothing, but he who closes his eyes to them receives many curses. [1]

Galatians 2:10: [10]All they asked was that we should continue to remember the poor, the very thing I was eager to do. [1]

I Timothy 6:17: [17]Command those who are rich in this present world not to be arrogant nor to put their hope in wealth, which is so uncertain, but to put their hope in God, who richly provides us with everything for our enjoyment. [18]Command them to do good, to be rich in good deeds, and to be generous and willing to share. [19]In this way they will lay up treasure for themselves as a firm foundation for the coming age, so that they may take hold of the life that is truly life. [1] *Please show me, sweet Holy Spirit, if I've begun to trust in my income or savings or retirement instead of You. Convict me to be radical in my giving so I can receive Your reward and have my heart fixed on You and the eternal.*

I John 3:17: [17]If anyone has material possessions and sees his brother in need but has no pity on him, how can the love of God be in him? [18]Dear children, let us not love with words or tongue, but with actions and in truth. [1]

26.

FORGIVENESS

The Word teaches us that our forgiveness of others is a prerequisite for our receiving forgiveness from the Lord and being right with Him. Nothing can block our receiving promises from the Lord like unforgiveness. He does not bless us because He owes us anything, but because He is a giver and loves us greatly. He loved us so much that He gave His Son. He has forgiven us of so much, at the greatest cost. We are called to model that forgiveness for others, partly because of our understanding of His great mercy shown to us. When we refuse to forgive others, the word says (in Matt. 6:15) that our Father will not forgive us. Certainly that dims or cuts off the most precious thing we have—our intimate fellowship with God, and His presence. Our faith, spiritual confidence and many other of His greatest blessings flow out of His grace and His Spirit on us. The word also teaches that our unforgiveness looses the enemy into our lives (not a good way to receive prosperity or anything else, see Matthew 18:34 below).

Dear Lord Jesus, I acknowledge that in great love and mercy, and at great cost, You have extended forgiveness to me, just by my asking. I could never deserve Your forgiveness, or any of the many benefits of Your salvation. Lord, I agree with Your word, that the most horrible things someone could do to me would not compare with the greatness of my sin, and what my sin did to Your Son, Jesus. So, Lord, by an act of my will, I choose to forgive each person who has wronged me, to forgive his or her sins against me, large and small. Each time I remember the fault, help me to keep on forgiving. I acknowledge that I don't have the right to keep tabs on the wrongs done against me. Please do a work in my heart so that I can also forgive with my emotions. Heal the hurts in me so that when I remember the events in which I was wronged, they no longer cause any pain. Show me how I helped to cause the problem, and how I have failed in similar ways, or could fail but for your grace. I bless each person who has wronged me in any way. Give me opportunities to bless and minister to them in practical ways, and to go the extra mile so my heart will be healed and my joy restored.

Holy Spirit, please remind me of those whom I have offended, or who have wronged me and to whom I have not been restored or have not fully forgiven. I want to be able to look in the eye of every person who has come into my life, and know that there is nothing between us that I have not forgiven or made every effort to make right. I must know that I have done my part to restore things between us. In Jesus' name I pray, Amen.

Matthew 18:21-35: 21Then Peter came to Jesus and asked, "Lord, how many times shall I forgive my brother when he sins against me? Up to seven times?" 22Jesus answered, "I tell you, not seven times, but seventy-seven times. 23Therefore, the kingdom of heaven is like a king who wanted to settle accounts with his servants. 24As he began the settlement, a man who owed him ten thousand talents was brought to him. [25]Since he was not able to pay, the master ordered that he and his wife and his children and all that he had be sold to repay the debt. [26]The servant fell on his knees before him. 'Be patient with me,' he begged, 'and I will pay back everything.' [27]The servant's master took pity on him, canceled the debt and let him go. [28]But when that servant went out, he found one of his fellow servants who owed him a hundred denarii. He grabbed him and began to choke him. 'Pay back what you owe me!' he demanded.

[29]His fellow servant fell to his knees and begged him, 'Be patient with me, and I will pay you back.'

[30]But he refused. Instead, he went off and had the man thrown into prison until he could pay the debt. [31]When the other servants saw what had happened, they were greatly distressed and went and told their master everything that had happened. [32]Then the master called the servant in. 'You wicked servant,' he said, 'I canceled all that debt of yours because you begged me to. [33]Shouldn't you have had mercy on your fellow servant just as I had on you?' [34]In anger his master turned him over to the jailers to be tortured, until he should pay back all he owed. [35]This is how my heavenly Father will treat each of you unless you forgive your brother from your heart." [1]

Lord, I don't want to remain with the torturers, the enemies of my soul, any more! By Your grace, I forgive my brother and my sister, in Jesus' name.

Proverbs 25:21-22: [21]If your enemy is hungry, give him food to eat; and if he is thirsty, give him water to drink; [22]For you will heap burning coals on his head, and the LORD will reward you. [3]

Proverbs 28:13: [13]He who conceals his sins does not prosper, but whoever confesses and renounces them finds mercy. [1]

Remind me, Holy Spirit, of those I have wronged, whether they realized it or not, and give me the guts to make it right with them.

Matthew 6:15: [15]But if you do not forgive men their sins, your Father will not forgive your sins. [1]

Luke 17:3-4: [3]Be on your guard! If your brother sins, rebuke him; and if he repents, forgive him. [4]And if he sins against you seven times a day, and returns to you seven times, saying, 'I repent,' forgive him. [3]

Luke 7:41-43: [41]"There was a certain creditor who had two debtors. One owed five hundred denarii, and the other fifty. [42]And when they had nothing with which to repay, he freely forgave them both. Tell Me, therefore, which of them will love him more?" [43]Simon answered and said, "I suppose the *one* whom he forgave more." And He said to him, "You have rightly judged." [2]

You have forgiven me of much, Lord, and I love and praise You for it!

· · · · · · · · · · ·

THE TESTIMONY OF John

Blessings begin with the simple phrase, "Forgive me." I remember so well how my family's lives changed so dramatically back in 1980 while living and ministering in Salina, Kansas.

After I had spoken to a group of church folks, a young man with the gifts of God walked up to me and asked, "What is your real name?" I was thirty years old and had been called Larry all my life, even though my legal name was John, same as my dad's. I was raised in a Christian home, but there was a lot of bickering and fighting between my parents. My mother openly admitted that she had never loved him. When I was born, my dad wanted to name me John, but she, in rebellion, wanted to name me Larry, and always called me that.

In 1980, when this young man walked up to me and asked my real name, I responded with the name I grew up with, Larry. He continued to ask. It was then that I told him my legal name was John, with no middle name, but I went by Larry. He responded, "I knew it. God told me to tell you that you are not going by your real name and if you repent, God will bring great blessing to your life."

I thought to myself, "This is crazy. God doesn't really care what name I go by as long as I live for Him." Later, after sharing this with my wife, she told me that she agreed with the word and that she knew that I had bitterness towards my dad. The next day, I went to my prayer closet and through many tears confessed the bitterness towards my earthly father. The Lord changed my heart completely. I wanted to share this with my parents and had the opportunity face to face a few weeks later.

We were moving to Houston, Texas, and stopped off in Dallas to visit my parents on the way.

I told my parents about my experience and asked my dad to forgive me for being bitter towards him, and told him that I loved him. He began to tear up. My mother had a different reaction. She let me know then that she had named me Larry from birth and that was that. Then she turned and left the room. I went to her and informed her that this was of God and that I loved her too, but that I was going to go with my legal name.

We continued on to Houston and had been there about two weeks when my mother called me. She was so excited that at first it was hard to understand what she was trying to say. She began to share with me that the night before she had decided to leave my dad forever, and was sleeping in another room. She explained that during the night she had been afflicted with a severe migraine headache and could not get relief even after constantly asking God to deliver her. She said that God spoke to her to go to her husband and she would be healed. She obeyed and went into his room to ask him to pray. When he did, she was instantly delivered from the migraine. She then began to repent to God for never loving her husband, asking Him to give her the love he deserved. God answered her and flooded her heart with a love she had never known before. She said it was like they had just started over again after forty years and were both totally in love with each other. She finished the conversation with telling me that because of my obedience to God, our family was unified for the first time. From that time on she called me "Son John" until she went to be with the Lord this past June.

Looking back, I can say that 1980 was a major turning point for us; we have received too many great blessings since to mention them individually here. My relationships with my mom, and especially my dad, have been very close over the years since. They moved to Alabama fifteen years ago to be with us in our ministry here and have blessed us with 76 acres of land to live on, and have given us years of joy. I know that if I had rejected God's word back in 1980, my life would have been completely different. Bitterness and hurt will never bring anything but sadness and death. Leave it at the altar—forgive and obey God, and be blessed. (Acts 8:21-24)

27.

THANKSGIVING

Many of our natural emotional responses, particularly as parents, reflect the heart of the Father. Few things bless the heart of a parent more than a child who is grateful and expresses thanks for things both new and old. That is the child we naturally want to bless with even more. Yet our fleshly nature is to appreciate the new, quickly take it for granted as the newness wears off, and start asking for more. The same attitude in our own children tends to hold us back from giving to them.

In America, we are blessed with literally thousands of blessings that would be considered great opulence in a third-world nation. We have wonderful roads and highways, a telephone system that almost always works, great food, fast food when we need it, air-conditioning and heat in our homes, indoor plumbing with running hot water, and soft toilet paper. We have access to books, internet and radio, and television programming brimming with spiritual insights and revelation. Most of us have access to fellowship with other believers who really love us and love the Lord. All these and so many more are wonderful blessings from the Lord. Make a habit to develop a grateful heart by developing a heart (a mouth) that is always thankful. When we speak thankfulness, our hearts respond, and we realize how much (more) we have to be thankful for.

Lord, I'm sorry for failing to be grateful for all the wonderful blessings You have given me. First of all, thank You for sending Jesus to show me Yourself and Your heart, and to purchase my wonderful salvation. Thank you for the body of Christ, and for all the wonderful people You've placed in my life. I know everything good in me has come from You, and through those You placed around me to help me. Thank You for allowing testing and hard times to come to bring character in my life and to give me a testimony of Your grace, mercy and faithfulness. How could I go on without Your love in my heart and Your hand on my life? You have also blessed me with great natural abundance. Forgive me for when I have so concentrated on what I don't have and what I want, that I have not been thankful for all the things You have given me. Thank you for supplying food and clothing, and so many other needs (and even wants) that I have had. You have been more than good to me. I place my other desires on the altar now and just thank and worship You for the great love You have lavished on me. I believe You will supply my real needs and bless me in Your time and Your way. I choose to wait on You with an attitude of gratefulness. I need Your help. In Jesus' name I pray, Amen.

I Thessalonians 5:16-18: 16Rejoice always; 17pray without ceasing; 18**in everything give thanks**; for this is God's will for you in Christ Jesus. [3]

Philippians 4:6: 6Do not be anxious about anything, but in everything, by prayer and petition, **with thanksgiving**, present your requests to God. [1]

Lord, forgive me for worrying about the things I need, instead of looking to You for them, asking in faith, and giving thanks for Your continual care for me. I love you, Lord.

Psalms 107:31-38: ³¹Oh, that *men* would **give thanks to the LORD** *for* His goodness, and *for* His wonderful works to the children of men! ³²Let them exalt Him also in the assembly of the people, and praise Him in the company of the elders. ³³He turns rivers into a wilderness, and the watersprings into dry ground; ³⁴A fruitful land into barrenness, for the wickedness of those who dwell in it. ³⁵He turns a wilderness into pools of water, and dry land into water-springs. ³⁶There He makes the hungry dwell, that they may establish a city for a dwelling place, ³⁷And sow fields and plant vineyards, that they may yield a fruitful harvest. ³⁸He also blesses them, and they multiply greatly; and He does not let their cattle decrease. 2

I Chronicles 29:11-16: ¹¹Yours, O LORD, *is* the greatness, the power and the glory, the victory and the majesty; for all *that is* in heaven and in earth *is Yours;* Yours *is* the kingdom, O LORD, and You are exalted as head over all. ¹²Both riches and honor *come* from You, and You reign over all. In Your hand *is* power and might; In Your hand *it is* to make great and to give strength to all. ¹³Now therefore, our God, **We thank You** and praise Your glorious name. ¹⁴But who *am* I, and who *are* my people, that we should be able to offer so willingly as this? For all things *come* from You, and of Your own we have given You. ¹⁵For we *are* aliens and pilgrims before You, as *were* all our fathers; Our days on earth *are* as a shadow, and without hope ¹⁶O LORD our God, all this abundance that we have prepared to build You a house for Your holy name is from Your hand, and *is* all Your own.²

Psalms 30:4-5: ⁴Sing praise to the LORD, you saints of His, and **give thanks** at the remembrance of His holy name. ⁵For His anger *is but for* a moment, His favor *is for* life; weeping may endure for a night, but joy *comes* in the morning.²

Psalms 35:18: ¹⁸**I will give You thanks** in the great assembly; I will praise You among many people.²

Psalms 50:14: [14]Offer to God **thanksgiving**, and pay your vows to the Most High.[2]

Psalms 107:1-2: [1]Oh, **give thanks to the LORD**, for *He is* good! For His mercy *endures* forever. [2]Let the redeemed of the LORD say *so,* whom He has redeemed from the hand of the enemy, [2]

Isaiah 12:3-6: [3]Therefore you will joyously draw water from the springs of salvation. [4]And in that day you will say, "**Give thanks to the LORD,** call on His name. Make known His deeds among the peoples; make *them* remember that His name is exalted." [5]Praise the LORD in song, for He has done excellent things; let this be known throughout the earth. [6]Cry aloud and shout for joy, O inhabitant of Zion, for great in your midst is the Holy One of Israel. [3]

Daniel 6:10: [10]Now when Daniel knew that the writing was signed, he went home. And in his upper room, with his windows open toward Jerusalem, he knelt down on his knees three times that day, and prayed and **gave thanks before his God, as was his custom since early days**. [2]

Matthew 11:25: [25]At that time Jesus answered and said, "**I thank You, Father**, Lord of heaven and earth, that You have hidden these things from *the* wise and prudent and have revealed them to babes. [2]

Ephesians 5:18b-20: [18b]...be filled with the Spirit, [19]speaking to one another in psalms and hymns and spiritual songs, singing and making melody in your heart to the Lord, [20]**giving thanks always for all things to God the Father in the name of our Lord Jesus Christ**[2]

Revelations 7:11-12: [11]All the angels stood around the throne and the elders and the four living creatures, and fell on their faces before the throne and worshiped God, [12]saying: "Amen! Blessing and glory and wisdom, **thanksgiving** and honor and power and might, *be* to **our God forever and ever**. Amen." [2]

(Emphases mine.)

APPENDIX 1

HEALING SCRIPTURES

1. HEALING

My Heavenly Father has healed me through the stripes of Jesus. Therefore, by Jesus' stripes I am healed from the top of my head to the tip of my toes. Thank You, Jesus, for healing me!!!

3 John 1:2: Beloved, I pray that you may prosper in all things and be in health, just as your soul prospers. [2]

Psalms 103:2-5: Bless the LORD, O my soul, and forget not all His benefits: [3]Who forgives all your iniquities, Who heals all your diseases, [4]Who redeems your life from destruction, Who crowns you with loving kindness and tender mercies, [5]Who satisfies your mouth with good *things, so that* your youth is renewed like the eagle's. [2]

Matthew 8:16, 17: [16]When evening had come, they brought to Him many who were demon-possessed. And He cast out the spirits with a word, and healed all who were sick, [17]that it might be fulfilled which was spoken by Isaiah the prophet, saying:
"He Himself took our infirmities and bore our sicknesses." [2]

Psalms 107:20: He sent His word and healed them, and delivered *them* from their destructions. [2]

John 10:10: The thief does not come except to steal, and to kill, and to destroy. I have come that they may have life, and that they may have *it* more abundantly. [2]

Hebrews 13:8: Jesus Christ *is* the same yesterday, today, and forever. [2]

Exodus 15:26: And said, "If you diligently heed the voice of the LORD your God and do what is right in His sight, give ear to His commandments and keep all His statutes, I will put none of the diseases on you which I have brought on the Egyptians. For I *am* the LORD who heals you." [2]

2. PROMISES

Jesus is the same as He was yesterday. If He healed in Matthew, Mark, Luke, and John, He will heal today and tomorrow. Thank You, Jesus, for healing me!!!

2 Corinthians 1:20: For all the promises of God in Him *are* Yes, and in Him Amen, to the glory of God through us. [2]

Romans 4:21: ...and being fully convinced that what He had promised He was also able to perform. [2]

Numbers 23:19: God *is* not a man, that He should lie, nor a son of man, that He should repent. Has He said, and will He not do? Or has He spoken, and will He not make it good? [2]

Hebrews 10:23: Let us hold fast the confession of *our* hope without wavering, for He who promised *is* faithful. [2]

Hebrews 11:11: By faith Sarah herself also received strength to conceive seed, and she bore a child when she was past the age, because she judged Him faithful who had promised. [2]

Romans 15:13: Now may the God of hope fill you with all joy and peace in believing, that you may abound in hope by the power of the Holy Spirit. [2]

3. TONGUE

The words of my Father tell me what I say. Death and life are in the power of the tongue. I make a decision to speak life to my mind and

*body. I speak to that mountain of sickness (specifically_____)
and say, "Leave my mind and body now in Jesus' name!"*

Proverbs 16:23-24: The heart of the wise teaches his mouth, and adds learning to his lips. [24]Pleasant words *are like* a honeycomb, sweetness to the soul and health to the bones. [2]

Proverbs 18:20-21: A man's stomach shall be satisfied from the fruit of his mouth; *from* the produce of his lips he shall be filled. [21]Death and life *are* in the power of the tongue, and those who love it will eat its fruit. [2]

Proverbs 6:2: You are snared by the words of your mouth; you are taken by the words of your mouth. [2]

Proverbs 12:18: There is one who speaks like the piercings of a sword, but the tongue of the wise *promotes* health. [2]

Job 22:28: You will also declare a thing, and it will be established for you; so light will shine on your ways. [2]

Matthew 12:37: For by your words you will be justified, and by your words you will be condemned. [2]

Mark 11:23: For assuredly, I say to you, whoever says to this mountain, 'Be removed and be cast into the sea,' and does not doubt in his heart, but believes that those things he says will be done; he will have whatever he says. [2]

Proverbs 14:3: In the mouth of a fool *is* a rod of pride, but the lips of the wise will preserve them. [2]

4. HEALING

I will hold fast to my confession of faith until my healing and deliverance is complete. I will not waiver until every cell, organ, gland, nerve, tissue and body system functions the way God created them to function. I hold fast to this confession. I have it now in Jesus' name!!!

I Peter 2:24: Who Himself bore our sins in His own body on the tree, that we, having died to sins, might live for righteousness—by whose stripes you were healed. [2]

Jeremiah 30:17: For I will restore health to you and heal you of your wounds,' says the LORD, 'Because they called you an outcast *saying:* "This *is* Zion; no one seeks her."' [2]

Acts 10:38: How God anointed Jesus of Nazareth with the Holy Spirit and with power, who went about doing good and healing all who were oppressed by the devil, for God was with Him. [2]

Proverbs 4:20-22: My son, give attention to my words; incline your ear to my sayings.
[21]Do not let them depart from your eyes; Keep them in the midst of your heart;
[22]For they are life to those who find them, and health to all their flesh. [2]

Matthew 12:15: But when Jesus knew *it,* He withdrew from there. And great multitudes followed Him, and He healed them all. [2]

Galatians 3:13-14: Christ has redeemed us from the curse of the law, having become a curse for us (for it is written, *"Cursed is everyone who hangs on a tree"*), [14]that the blessing of Abraham might come upon the Gentiles in Christ Jesus, that we might receive the promise of the Spirit through faith. [2]

5. GUIDANCE

My steps are ordered by the Lord, because He promised to guide me into all truth for His kingdom, which will cause me to be blessed. My steps are directed by God.

Psalms 119:11: Your word I have hidden in my heart, that I might not sin against You. [2]

Jeremiah 10:23: O LORD, I know the way of man *is* not in himself; *it is* not in man who walks to direct his own steps. 2

Psalms 32:8: I will instruct you and teach you in the way you should go; I will guide you with My eye. 2

Psalms 48:14: For this *is* God, Our God forever and ever; He will be our guide *even* to death. 2

Psalms 25:9: The humble He guides in justice, and the humble He teaches His way. 2

Proverbs 3:5-6: Trust in the LORD with all your heart, and lean not on your own understanding; 6In all your ways acknowledge Him, and He shall direct your paths. 2

John 16:13-15: However, when He, the Spirit of truth, has come, He will guide you into all truth; for He will not speak on His own *authority,* but whatever He hears He will speak; and He will tell you things to come. 14He will glorify Me, for He will take of what is Mine and declare *it* to you. 15All things that the Father has are Mine. Therefore I said that He will take of Mine and declare *it* to you. 2

Jeremiah 17:5-6: Thus says the LORD: "Cursed *is* the man who trusts in man and makes flesh his strength, whose heart departs from the LORD. 6For he shall be like a shrub in the desert, and shall not see when good comes, but shall inhabit the parched places in the wilderness, *in* a salt land *which is* not inhabited. 2

Psalms 5:8: Lead me, O LORD, in Your righteousness because of my enemies; make Your way straight before my face. 2

6. STRENGTH

A right relationship with my heavenly Father produces divine strength in me that is far superior to my natural strength. I trust the Lord to give me strength from within.

Psalms 46:1: God *is* our refuge and strength, a very present help in trouble. 2

Psalms 90:10: The days of our lives *are* seventy years; and if by reason of strength *they are* eighty years, yet their boast *is* only labor and sorrow; for it is soon cut off, and we fly away. 2

Habakkuk 3:19: The LORD God is my strength; He will make my feet like deer's *feet,* and He will make me walk on my high hills. . . . 2

Proverbs 10:29: The way of the LORD *is* strength for the upright, but destruction *will come* to the workers of iniquity. 2

Isaiah 26:4: Trust in the LORD forever, for in YAH, the LORD, *is* everlasting strength. 2

Nehemiah 8:10: Then he said to them, "Go your way, eat the fat, drink the sweet, and send portions to those for whom nothing is prepared; for *this* day *is* holy to our Lord. Do not sorrow, for the joy of the LORD is your strength." 2

Isaiah 12:2: Behold, God *is* my salvation, I will trust and not be afraid; 'For YAH, the LORD, *is* my strength and song; He also has become my salvation.' 2

Psalms 103:5: Who satisfies your mouth with good *things, so that* your youth is renewed like the eagle's. 2

7. LONG LIFE

Sickness and disease, I bind you in the name of Jesus. You have no legal right to stay in my home, so in Jesus' name, leave now! I claim _____ healing and deliverance in Jesus' name. There is long life in my home, not sickness and disease. Thank You, Jesus!!!

Psalms 91:16: With long life I will satisfy him, and show him My salvation. 2

Psalms 90:10: The days of our lives *are* seventy years; and if by reason of strength *they are* eighty years, yet their boast *is* only labor and sorrow; for it is soon cut off, and we fly away. [2]

Proverbs 4:10: Hear, my son, and receive my sayings, and the years of your life will be many. [2]

Proverbs 3:1-2: My son, do not forget my law, but let your heart keep my commands; [2]For length of days and long life and peace they will add to you. [2]

Proverbs 3:13: Happy *is* the man *who* finds wisdom, and the man *who* gains understanding;[2]

Proverbs 3:16: Length of days *is* in her right hand; in her left hand riches and honor. [2]

8. HEALING

Jesus took my infirmities and bore my sicknesses. Therefore, I am totally and completely healed. Body, you come in line with the word of God in the name of Jesus! I command you to function correctly in Jesus' name. Weakness, _____, _____, _____, leave this mind and body in Jesus' name!!!

Exodus 23:25-26: So you shall serve the LORD your God, and He will bless your bread and your water. And I will take sickness away from the midst of you. [26]No one shall suffer miscarriage or be barren in your land; I will fulfill the number of your days. [2]

Mark 16:17-18: And these signs will follow those who believe: In My name they will cast out demons; they will speak with new tongues; [18]they will take up serpents; and if they drink anything deadly, it will by no means hurt them; they will lay hands on the sick, and they will recover. [2]

Psalms 105:37: He also brought them out with silver and gold, and *there was* none feeble among His tribes. [2]

Numbers 23:19: God *is* not a man, that He should lie, nor a son of man, that He should repent. Has He said, and will He not do? Or has He spoken, and will He not make it good? [2]

9. PROTECTION

God's angels encamp about me and my family. No evil shall come upon me, because I abide under the shadow of my God and God alone is my refuge and my fortress. (Read Psalm 91 often.)

Psalms 121:7-8: The LORD shall preserve you from all evil; He shall preserve your soul. [8]The LORD shall preserve your going out and your coming in from this time forth, and even forevermore. [2]

Psalms 34:7: The angel of the LORD encamps all around those who fear Him, and delivers them. [2]

Psalms 145:20: The LORD preserves all who love Him, but all the wicked He will destroy. [2]

Proverbs 2:8: He guards the paths of justice, and preserves the way of His saints. [2]

Proverbs 30:5: Every word of God *is* pure; He *is* a shield to those who put their trust in Him. [2]

Proverbs 11:8: The righteous is delivered from trouble, and it comes to the wicked instead. [2]

Psalms 91:10-11: No evil shall befall you, nor shall any plague come near your dwelling; [11]For He shall give His angels charge over you, to keep you in all your ways. [2]

Proverbs 2:10-11: When wisdom enters your heart, and knowledge is pleasant to your soul, [11]Discretion will preserve you; understanding will keep you, [2]

John 17:15: I do not pray that You should take them out of the world, but that You should keep them from the evil one. [2]

10. HEALING

I forbid any sickness or disease to come upon my body. Every disease, bacteria and virus that touches this body dies instantly in the name of Jesus. My body is chemically balanced in Jesus' name. The metabolism in my body is normal in Jesus' name.

Hebrews 13:8: Jesus Christ *is* the same yesterday, today, and forever. [2]

Matthew 8:16: When evening had come, they brought to Him many who were demon-possessed. And He cast out the spirits with a word, and healed all who were sick. [2]

Matthew 12:14-15: [14]Then the Pharisees went out and plotted against Him, how they might destroy Him. [15]But when Jesus knew *it,* He withdrew from there. And great multitudes followed Him, and He healed them all. [2]

Luke 6:19: And the whole multitude sought to touch Him, for power went out from Him and healed *them* all. [2]

Matthew 15:30-31: [30]Then great multitudes came to Him, having with them *the* lame, blind, mute, maimed, and many others; and they laid them down at Jesus' feet, and He healed them. [31]So the multitude marveled when they saw *the* mute speaking, *the* maimed made whole, *the* lame walking, and *the* blind seeing; and they glorified the God of Israel. [2]

Luke 4:40: When the sun was setting, all those who had any that were sick with various diseases brought them to Him; and He laid His hands on every one of them and healed them. [2]

11. HOLY SPIRIT

I can use my mind to get information about healing and health, but only the Holy Spirit can quicken and make it work in my life. Thank God, this is the Holy Spirit's ministry and He will make it work in and for me.

John 14:26: But the Helper, the Holy Spirit, whom the Father will send in My name, He will teach you all things, and bring to your remembrance all things that I said to you. [2]

John 16:13-14: However, when He, the Spirit of truth, has come, He will guide you into all truth; for He will not speak on His own *authority,* but whatever He hears He will speak; and He will tell you things to come. [14]He will glorify Me, for He will take of what is Mine and declare *it* to you. [2]

John 6:63: It is the Spirit who gives life; the flesh profits nothing. The words that I speak to you are spirit, and *they* are life. [2]

Romans 8:14: For as many as are led by the Spirit of God, these are sons of God. [2]

John 14:16-17: And I will pray the Father, and He will give you another Helper, that He may abide with you forever—[17]the Spirit of truth, whom the world cannot receive, because it neither sees Him nor knows Him; but you know Him, for He dwells with you and will be in you. [2]

Acts 10:38: How God anointed Jesus of Nazareth with the Holy Spirit and with power, who went about doing good and healing all who were oppressed by the devil, for God was with Him. [2]

Galatians 4:6: And because you are sons, God has sent forth the Spirit of His Son into your hearts, crying out, "Abba, Father!" [2]

12. FORGIVENESS

I refuse to walk in strife or resentment against anyone. I refuse to carry grudges or dislike anybody. I am a quick forgiver and a quick believer in God's work. I forgive because my heavenly Father tells me to forgive.

Psalms 66:18: If I regard iniquity in my heart, the Lord will not hear. 2

Mark 11:25-26: And whenever you stand praying, if you have anything against anyone, forgive him, that your Father in heaven may also forgive you your trespasses. 26But if you do not forgive, neither will your Father in heaven forgive your trespasses. 2

Matthew 6:14-15: For if you forgive men their trespasses, your heavenly Father will also forgive you. 15But if you do not forgive men their trespasses, neither will your Father forgive your trespasses. 2

Luke 6:36-37: Therefore be merciful, just as your Father also is merciful. 37Judge not, and you shall not be judged. Condemn not, and you shall not be condemned. Forgive, and you will be forgiven. 2

Matthew 18:32-35: Then his master, after he had called him, said to him, 'You wicked servant! I forgave you all that debt because you begged me. 33Should you not also have had compassion on your fellow servant, just as I had pity on you?' 34And his master was angry, and delivered him to the torturers until he should pay all that was due to him.
35So My heavenly Father also will do to you if each of you, from his heart, does not forgive his brother his trespasses. 2

13. HEALING

I overcome sickness and disease by the blood of the Lamb (Jesus), and the word of my testimony. Devil, you take your sickness and disease and leave my body right now. I rebuke you from me in the name of Jesus. Father, I return Your word to You—by Jesus' stripes I am healed, by Jesus' stripes I am healed, by Jesus' stripes I am healed!

John 10:10: The thief does not come except to steal, and to kill, and to destroy. I have come that they may have life, and that they may have *it* more abundantly. [2]

James 1:6-8: But let him ask in faith, with no doubting, for he who doubts is like a wave of the sea driven and tossed by the wind. [7]For let not that man suppose that he will receive anything from the Lord; [8]*he is* a double-minded man, unstable in all his ways. [2]

Acts 10:38: How God anointed Jesus of Nazareth with the Holy Spirit and with power, who went about doing good and healing all who were oppressed by the devil, for God was with Him. [2]

Matthew 6:10: Your kingdom come. Your will be done on earth as *it is* in heaven. [2]

14. HUMILITY

Any failure is on my part, never my God who cannot fail. Father, in Jesus' name, create in me a humble heart as my Savior had. I want to be and can be like Jesus. [2]

John 14:12-14: Most assuredly, I say to you, he who believes in Me, the works that I do he will do also; and greater *works* than these he will do, because I go to My Father. [13]And whatever you ask in My name, that I will do, that the Father may be glorified in the Son. [14]If you ask anything in My name, I will do *it*. [2]

John 5:30: I can of Myself do nothing. As I hear, I judge; and My judgment is righteous, because I do not seek My own will, but the will of the Father who sent Me. [2]

John 5:19: Then Jesus answered and said to them, "Most assuredly, I say to you, the Son can do nothing of Himself, but what He sees the Father do; for whatever He does, the Son also does in like manner." 2

James 4:10: Humble yourselves in the sight of the Lord, and He will lift you up. 2

Colossians 3:12-13: Therefore, as *the* elect of God, holy and beloved, put on tender mercies, kindness, humility, meekness, longsuffering; 13bearing with one another, and forgiving one another, if anyone has a complaint against another; even as Christ forgave you, so you also *must do.* 2

Luke 18:14: I tell you, this man went down to his house justified *rather* than the other; for everyone who exalts himself will be humbled, and he who humbles himself will be exalted. 2

Proverbs 18:12: Before destruction the heart of a man is haughty, and before honor *is* humility. 2

Proverbs 22:4: By humility *and* the fear of the LORD *are* riches and honor and life. 2

15. PSALM 91 (for personal confession)

1He who dwells in the secret place of the Most High Shall abide under the shadow of the Almighty. 2I will say of the LORD, "*He is* my refuge and my fortress; My God, in Him I will trust." 3Surely He shall deliver you from the snare of the fowler *and* from the perilous pestilence. 4He shall cover you with His feathers, and under His wings you shall take refuge; His truth *shall be your* shield and buckler. 5You shall not be afraid of the terror by night, *nor* of the arrow *that* flies by day, 6Nor of the pestilence *that* walks in darkness, *nor* of the destruction *that* lays waste at noonday. 7A thousand may fall at your side, and ten thousand at your right hand; *but* it shall not come near you. 8Only with your eyes shall you look, and see the reward of the wicked. [9]Because you have made the LORD, *who is* my refuge, *even* the Most High, your dwelling place, [10]No evil shall befall you, nor shall any plague come near your dwelling; [11]For He shall give His angels charge over you, to keep you in all your ways. [12]In *their* hands they shall bear you up, lest you dash your foot against a stone. [13]You shall tread upon the lion and the cobra, the young lion and the serpent you shall trample underfoot. [14]"Because he has set his love upon Me, therefore I will deliver him I will set him on high, because he has known My name. [15]He shall call upon Me, and I will answer him; I *will be* with him in trouble; I will deliver him and honor him.[16]With long life I will satisfy him, and show him My salvation."

2

APPENDIX 2

The translations used in this work are referenced by superscripts to emphasize the word of God, not the translation. This is the key.

New International Version ([1]) – 1

New King James Version ([2]) – 2

New American Standard ([3]) – 3

King James ([4]) – 4

Amplified Version ([5]) – 5

CPSIA information can be obtained at www.ICGtesting.com
Printed in the USA
LVOW072210221212

312918LV00001B/35/P